AF413517

MODI AND INDIA'S UNRESOLVED CONTRADICTIONS

AMARENDRA REDDY SAGILA

Dedicated to my beloved father, Sri Rami Reddy Sagila
(1953-2000)

Who planted the seeds of curiosity

Nurtured my love for reading, and

Taught me to think deeply about the world

Your wisdom continues to guide me!

Contents

Contents

Contents

Preface

My journey with India's political economy began not in the halls of academia, but in the streets of Hyderabad. As a young engineering graduate filled with idealism and dreams of a resurgent India, I found myself drawn to the Lok Satta Party in Andhra Pradesh, a movement that promised rational, reform-oriented politics. Leading the election campaign in 2009 for the Malkajgiri Assembly constituency, where our candidate secured over 20,000 votes, I experienced firsthand both the possibilities and limitations of political reform in India.

This book emerges from that unique vantage point – of someone who has straddled multiple worlds. From my early days as a grassroots political activist to my current position as a professional in Virginia, USA, I have maintained a deep engagement with India's development challenges. My engineering background has perhaps influenced my approach to analyzing India's problems: a focus on systems, root causes, and structural solutions rather than superficial fixes.

The years since my direct involvement in politics have given me both distance and perspective. Working in the United States while maintaining close ties to India has allowed me to observe India's transformation through a distinctive lens. This position offers both the advantage of detachment and the continuing emotional investment of someone who dreams of India's potential.

The chapters that follow examine several interconnected themes that I believe are crucial to understanding contemporary India. We explore how the BJP under Modi has achieved unprecedented political dominance while showing surprising hesitancy in pursuing dramatic economic reforms. We analyze why socialist ideas maintain their grip on Indian political discourse even as the country embraces aspects of market economics. We look at how Hindu nationalism has reshaped Indian politics while often failing to address the fundamental challenges of governance and development.

My early experiences with Lok Satta Party taught me something crucial about India: the gap between what is necessary and what is politically feasible is often vast. This understanding informs the book's analysis of why India, despite its enormous potential and periodic waves of reform, continues to struggle with implementing comprehensive changes.

This is not primarily a book about Modi the individual, though his influence pervades every chapter. Rather, it is an attempt to understand the India that produced Modi, the India that he has helped shape, and the India that will exist long after his tenure. It examines how historical grievances, economic aspirations, and cultural dynamics have combined to create the current moment in Indian politics.

The analysis draws on my unique perspective as someone who has been both an insider and outsider to India's political process. It combines personal observations with detailed examination of policy documents, electoral data, and economic indicators. However, the goal is not merely to present data or chronicle events, but to understand the deeper currents shaping India's trajectory.

Some readers may find aspects of this analysis challenging. Those who see Modi as India's savior may bristle at the examination of his government's limitations. Those who view him primarily as a threat to India's secular fabric may be uncomfortable with the discussion of legitimate grievances that have fueled his rise. However, India's challenges – and opportunities – are too important to be viewed through the lens of partisan positions.

As someone who once harbored dreams of transforming India through direct political action, I now offer this analysis as a different kind of contribution to India's development discourse. My hope is that this book will help readers understand why India's much-needed reforms remain elusive and what might be done to advance them.

This book is written in the belief that understanding India's contradictions is crucial not just for Indians but for anyone interested in the future of democracy and development in our complex world. As India navigates the challenges ahead, the choices it makes will resonate far beyond its borders. My hope is that this analysis contributes to a deeper understanding of these choices and their implications.

The story of India's struggle with reform is still being written. Understanding the forces that have shaped this struggle is crucial for charting a path forward. It is to this task that we now turn.

About The Author

Amarendra Reddy Sagila brings together a unique combination of technical expertise, business education, and grassroots political experience to analyze contemporary India. Even while working as a Data Governance Analyst in the IT sector in Ashburn, Virginia, he remains profoundly connected to India's political and economic development, viewing it through the lens of someone who has experienced both Indian and American systems.

His journey began as an engineering graduate in India, where early idealism led him to active participation in political reform. As the campaign leader for the Lok Satta Party in the Malkajgiri Assembly constituency in Andhra Pradesh, he helped secure over 20,000 votes for the party's candidate in 2009, gaining firsthand experience in the challenges of implementing reform-oriented politics in India.

Amar holds an engineering degree from JNTU Hyderabad and an MBA in Finance from the State University of New York at Buffalo. This interdisciplinary background enables him to analyze India's challenges through multiple lenses – technical, financial, and political.

After transitioning to a career in technology, Amar has continued to study and analyze India's political economy. He brings both an engineer's systematic approach and a financial analyst's perspective to understanding the complex interplay of forces shaping modern India. His professional background in data governance adds analytical rigor to his examination of India's institutional challenges and reform possibilities.

Currently based in Ashburn, Virginia, Amar combines his technical career with ongoing engagement in India's development discourse. He offers a perspective that bridges the practical and the theoretical, the local and the global, in analyzing India's trajectory.

Amarendra Reddy Sagila

The Modi Phenomenon and Hindu Nationalism

1. Minimum Reforms, Maximum Politics: Decoding Modi's India

2. The BJP's Transformation: From Political Fringe to National Dominance

3. Historical Grievances, Political Resurgence: The Hindu Nationalist Perspective

4. Hindu Nationalist Overreach

5. Modi's Electoral Success: A Victory for Reform or Corporate Interests?

୪୨

This section explores the rise of Narendra Modi, the BJP's dominance, and the ideological underpinnings of Hindu nationalism. It examines the political strategies, historical grievances, and the cultural and religious tensions that have shaped contemporary India.

I

Minimum Reforms, Maximum Politics: Decoding Modi's India

When Narendra Modi swept to power in 2014, his campaign was built on the promise of transformative economic reforms, minimal government intervention, and a corruption-free India. As his government approaches its twelfth year in power, a striking paradox has emerged: unprecedented political dominance has not translated into the bold economic reforms many had anticipated. This disconnect raises critical questions about India's economic trajectory and whether the country is leveraging its full potential under Modi's leadership.

The Infrastructure Success Story

One of the Modi government's most notable achievements has been its focus on infrastructure development. The pace of highway construction has accelerated dramatically, transforming India's road network and improving connectivity across the country. The digital revolution, spearheaded by initiatives like the Unified Payments Interface (UPI), has positioned India as a global leader in digital infrastructure. These advancements have not only modernized daily life for millions but also enhanced the ease of doing business in key sectors.

The Banking Sector Clean-up

Another significant accomplishment has been the resolution of non-performing assets (NPAs) in the banking sector. This long-overdue clean-up, though painful, has strengthened the financial system's foundation. By addressing the NPA crisis, the government has restored some confidence in India's banking sector, paving the way for more robust economic activity.

Foreign Policy and Security

On the foreign policy front, Modi's India has shown a newfound assertiveness, particularly in standing up to Chinese territorial aggression. This marks a departure from the more cautious approach of previous administrations and reflects a broader shift in India's geopolitical strategy. The government's focus on strengthening national security and forging strategic alliances has bolstered India's position on the global stage.

The Reform Deficit: A Missed Opportunity?

Despite these successes, the Modi government's record on core economic reforms has been underwhelming. The promise of "Minimum Government, Maximum Governance" has largely given way to increased regulation and state intervention. Key reforms, such as the privatization of public sector undertakings (PSUs) and state-owned banks—essential for improving efficiency and reducing government overreach—have seen minimal progress.

The concentration of economic power in a few corporate conglomerates, particularly the Adani and Ambani groups, has raised concerns about crony capitalism. The Adani group's control of major ports and the perceived protection of certain business interests through regulatory policies have fueled accusations of an uneven playing field. This trend undermines the government's stated commitment to fostering competition and innovation.

Foreign investment policies have also remained restrictive, particularly in sectors like retail. Companies like Walmart have faced significant hurdles, reflecting a protectionist approach that prioritizes domestic players over global competition. While this may shield local businesses in the short term, it risks stifling efficiency and long-term growth.

౩

The Institutional Challenge: Erosion of Trust?

Perhaps the most concerning aspect of Modi's governance has been the perceived weaponization of state institutions. Agencies like the Enforcement Directorate, Income Tax Department, and investigative bodies have been accused of targeting political opponents, while those aligned with the ruling party appear to enjoy immunity. While corruption at the ministerial level may have decreased, systemic corruption in government offices and state administrations persists. The selective application of anti-corruption measures has eroded public trust in these institutions, undermining the credibility of the government's reform agenda.

Critical Reforms Left Untouched

The government's reluctance to pursue fundamental reforms in key sectors like education, healthcare, and law enforcement is particularly troubling. These areas are critical for building human capital and improving governance, yet they remain largely unaddressed. Without comprehensive reforms, India's long-term growth potential could be severely constrained.

The Cultural and Religious Focus

Instead of prioritizing economic reforms, the Modi government has increasingly focused on cultural and religious issues that resonate with its core Hindu base. Initiatives like the construction of the Ram Mandir, the abrogation of Article 370 in Kashmir, and the push for a Uniform Civil Code have galvanized political support but have done little to address India's pressing economic challenges. While these moves have solidified Modi's electoral dominance, they risk diverting attention from the structural reforms needed to sustain growth.

The Return to Populism

Contrary to expectations of reduced government intervention, the Modi administration has embraced populist measures and welfare schemes. While social welfare is undeniably important, the growing culture of freebies across political parties threatens fiscal discipline and economic stability. This shift toward populism raises questions about the government's commitment to long-term economic reform.

ಜ

The Legacy Question: A Contrast with Past Reforms

The contrast with previous reform periods is stark. The 1991 economic liberalization under P.V. Narasimha Rao and Manmohan Singh, followed by Atal Bihari Vajpayee's reforms, transformed India's economy by reducing government control and fostering competition. Modi's government, despite its strong political mandate, has shown little appetite for similarly bold reforms. This hesitancy has left many wondering whether India is squandering a historic opportunity to achieve sustained high growth.

ಜ

Looking Ahead: The Path to Sustained Growth

The paradox of Modi's governance lies in its strong political position coupled with a hesitancy to pursue transformative economic reforms. While infrastructure development and digital advancements are commendable, they are not enough to address India's deeper structural challenges. To realize its full potential, India needs comprehensive reforms in education, healthcare, governance, and market structures.

The key question is whether political dominance without corresponding economic reforms can sustain India's growth aspirations. As global economic patterns shift and new challenges emerge, India must move beyond infrastructural improvements and digital advances. The government must channel its political capital into meaningful reforms that build human capital, enhance governance, and foster a competitive business environment.

ॐ

Conclusion: A Historic Opportunity at Risk

Modi's government still has the political strength to implement significant reforms. However, unless this strength is directed toward addressing India's structural challenges, the country risks missing a historic opportunity to achieve sustained high growth and comprehensive development. The true measure of political success should not be limited to electoral victories but should also include the creation of lasting institutional and economic frameworks that enhance India's global competitiveness and improve the living standards of its citizens.

In the end, the legacy of Modi's India will be judged not by its political dominance but by its ability to deliver on the promise of a modern, prosperous, and inclusive economy.

II

The BJP's Transformation: From Political Fringe to National Dominance

The Bharatiya Janata Party's (BJP) evolution from a peripheral political entity to India's dominant political force represents one of the most remarkable transformations in the nation's political history. While often portrayed as a gradual rise, the BJP was actually confined to the political fringes until the late 1980s, with its mainstreaming occurring in distinct phases. Under Prime Minister Narendra Modi's leadership, the party achieved unprecedented dominance that has fundamentally and irreversibly reshaped India's political landscape.

ॐ

The Early Years: A Fringe Player (1984-1990)

The BJP's beginnings were humble and geographically limited. Following its formation in 1980, the party remained confined largely to what is colloquially known as the "cow belt" - Hindi-speaking northern states. In the 1984 elections, the party secured just two seats in the Lok Sabha, marking its minimal national presence. During this period, the BJP struggled for political relevance, with the Indian National Congress and various regional parties dominating the political landscape. The party's Hindutva ideology was viewed as extreme by mainstream voters, keeping it on the political periphery.

ॐ

The Rath Yatra Movement: Breaking into the National Arena

The watershed moment came with Lal Krishna Advani's Rath Yatra in 1990, which dramatically expanded the BJP's influence by mobilizing support around the Ram Janmabhoomi movement. This strategic move tapped into the deep-rooted sentiments of India's Hindu majority regarding the Ram Mandir issue in Ayodhya. By bringing this culturally and emotionally significant issue to the forefront of national politics, Advani catapulted the BJP from the fringes into the mainstream political discourse.

The Ram Mandir issue resonated profoundly with millions of Hindus across the country, transcending regional and caste divides. By championing this cause, the BJP positioned itself as the political voice of Hindu cultural aspirations, significantly broadening its appeal beyond its traditional voter base. This marked the beginning of the

BJP's transformation from a marginal player to a significant national force.

The Vajpayee Era: Political Legitimacy Despite Being "Untouchable"

Atal Bihari Vajpayee's tenure as Prime Minister (1998–2004) represented the next critical phase in the BJP's evolution. Despite the party being considered something of a "political untouchable" by many regional parties until the late 1990s due to its Hindutva ideology, Vajpayee's moderate and inclusive approach helped overcome this barrier. His leadership style legitimized the BJP as a party capable of governing at the national level while building bridges with diverse political allies.

Vajpayee's coalition government demonstrated the BJP's ability to work within India's pluralistic framework, gaining acceptance among diverse sections of society. However, this period represented a compromise on core ideological positions rather than their mainstreaming, as evidenced by the party's need to temporarily shelve contentious issues to maintain coalition support. The BJP had to put aside its three main ideological pillars: the construction of Ram Mandir in Ayodhya, the abrogation of Article 370 that gave special status to Jammu and Kashmir, and the implementation of a Uniform Civil Code to replace religious personal laws. These issues, central to the BJP's Hindutva platform, were deliberately kept off the immediate governance agenda to maintain coalition stability with parties that opposed these positions.

Post-2004 Decline: Return to the Margins

The BJP's defeat in the 2004 and subsequent 2009 general elections revealed its limitations and temporarily halted its national ascendancy. The party won only 138 seats in 2004 and further declined to 116 seats in 2009, far below the 272 required for a parliamentary majority. This electoral setback highlighted the BJP's continuing struggle to transcend its image as a party primarily rooted in the Hindi heartland and Hindutva ideology.

During this period, the Congress-led UPA government dominated national politics, pushing the BJP back toward the political margins. It became clear that despite the progress made under Vajpayee, the party needed a new strategy and leadership to achieve genuine national dominance. The BJP remained significant but secondary in the national political arena.

ॐ

The Modi Revolution: Irreversible Mainstreaming of the BJP

Narendra Modi's emergence as the BJP's prime ministerial candidate in 2013 marked a decisive turning point in Indian politics. Unlike the accommodative approach of the Vajpayee era, Modi's leadership brought a transformative vision that fundamentally altered both the BJP's position and Indian politics as a whole.

ॐ

Ideological Mainstreaming and Hindu Consciousness

Under Modi, the BJP successfully shifted from moderating its Hindutva agenda to mainstreaming it. The party effectively awakened what many supporters describe as the "consciousness of the Hindu majority," normalizing cultural nationalism within political discourse. Initiatives like the abrogation of Article 370, the construction of the Ram Mandir in Ayodhya, and the implementation of the Citizenship Amendment Act (CAA) resonated with a large section of the Hindu electorate.

Unlike previous periods when such positions were considered extreme, Modi's BJP made Hindu cultural assertion a mainstream political position while simultaneously building resentment against what it termed "minority appeasement politics." This ideological shift represents perhaps the most profound and irreversible aspect of the BJP's transformation.

※

Organizational and Financial Dominance

Under Modi, the BJP has become India's wealthiest political party by far, leveraging electoral bonds and corporate donations to build a formidable war chest. This financial advantage has enabled sophisticated, data-driven election campaigns and maintenance of a robust organizational structure across the country. The BJP's membership has grown exponentially, making it one of the largest political organizations in the world and creating an institutional infrastructure that will outlast any single leadership.

※

Unprecedented Geographical Expansion

Modi's BJP has successfully expanded far beyond its traditional strongholds in the Hindi heartland, achieving what previous leadership could not – genuine national presence. The party has made remarkable inroads into the Northeast, forming governments in states like Assam, Manipur, and Tripura that were previously considered beyond its reach.

In southern India, the BJP has emerged as a key player in Karnataka and is making significant progress in Telangana, where it has risen to become the third strongest party. Even in states with strong regional identities like Tamil Nadu, Kerala, and Andhra Pradesh – once considered impenetrable for the BJP – the party has established and continues to build a meaningful presence. This pan-Indian footprint represents a fundamental shift from the party's formerly limited geographic appeal.

ॐ

Political Realignment and Coalition Dominance

The BJP's rise under Modi has redefined coalition politics in India. Once viewed with skepticism by regional parties due to its Hindutva agenda, the BJP has now become the preferred alliance partner for many. This shift reflects not just political opportunism but the party's growing acceptability and its ability to offer a winning platform. The National Democratic Alliance (NDA), led by the BJP, has emerged as a cohesive coalition, further solidifying the party's national dominance.

ॐ

Factors Behind the BJP's Irreversible Rise

Several factors have contributed to the BJP's unprecedented transformation under Modi, making its dominant position difficult to challenge in the foreseeable future:

- **Charismatic Leadership**: Modi's ability to connect with voters, his oratory skills, and his image as a decisive leader have been instrumental in expanding the party's appeal far beyond its traditional base.

- **Effective Communication Strategy:** The BJP has mastered modern political messaging, leveraging traditional media, social media, and Modi's personal brand to communicate its narrative and counter opposition critiques.
- **Fusion of Cultural Nationalism and Development:** Unlike previous iterations of right-wing politics, Modi's BJP has successfully combined cultural nationalism with promises of economic development, welfare schemes, and good governance.
- **Organizational Discipline:** The BJP's well-oiled organizational machinery, supported by RSS cadres, has given it a significant edge in voter mobilization and election management across diverse regions.
- **Opposition Fragmentation:** The decline of the Congress and the inability of regional parties to present a united front have further strengthened the BJP's position as the only party with genuine national reach.

౭ం

The New Indian Political Reality

The BJP's transformation under Modi represents more than just electoral success; it signifies a fundamental and irreversible shift in India's political and ideological landscape. The awakening of Hindu cultural consciousness that Modi has fostered cannot simply be reversed by electoral defeats or leadership changes. The BJP has replaced the Congress as the central pole of Indian politics, a position it appears likely to maintain in the foreseeable future due to:

- An institutionalized organizational infrastructure spanning the entire country
- Unmatched financial resources that dwarf opposition capabilities
- A broad geographical presence that continues to expand
- The mainstreaming of previously controversial ideological positions
- A deep connection with the cultural aspirations of the Hindu majority

ॐ

Conclusion

The Modi era has redefined Indian politics, transforming the BJP from a once-fringe political entity to the country's dominant political force. This transformation goes beyond electoral victories, reflecting a profound realignment of political ideologies and voter preferences that appears irreversible. The awakening of Hindu consciousness and the normalization of cultural nationalism within mainstream politics represent changes to India's political DNA rather than temporary shifts.

As India moves forward, the BJP's dominance under Modi will continue to shape the nation's political, social, and economic trajectory, leaving an indelible mark on its history. What began as a fringe movement has, through strategic evolution and transformative leadership, become the defining political force of contemporary India with an institutional strength and ideological resonance that suggests its dominance will extend well into the future.

III

Historical Grievances, Political Resurgence: The Hindu Nationalist Perspective

India's contemporary political landscape is shaped by a complex interplay of historical grievances, cultural identity, and transformative politics. The rise of Hindu nationalism, particularly under the Bharatiya Janata Party (BJP) and Prime Minister Narendra Modi's leadership, is deeply rooted in a historical narrative of perceived cultural marginalization that spans centuries. This resurgence is not merely a political movement but a cultural reawakening, reflecting the collective memory and aspirations of a significant portion of India's Hindu population.

ॐ

Historical Contexts of Cultural Trauma

The roots of Hindu nationalist sentiment can be traced back to the medieval period, marked by invasions and rule by Muslim dynasties, some of which were characterized by religious and cultural oppression. The 10th and 11th centuries saw invasions by figures like Mahmud of Ghazni and Muhammad of Ghor, who targeted Hindu temples and religious sites, initiating a prolonged era of cultural and religious conflict. While the Mughal Empire is often remembered for its contributions to art, architecture, and administration, certain rulers, such as Aurangzeb, are perceived as having imposed policies that marginalized Hindu communities.

Aurangzeb's reign, in particular, is often cited as a period of heightened religious intolerance. Historical accounts highlight the destruction of Hindu temples, such as the Kashi Vishwanath Temple in Varanasi and the Kesava Deo Temple in Mathura, and the imposition of the jizya tax on non-Muslims. These actions, coupled with narratives of forced conversions and the desecration of religious artifacts, entrenched a sense of generational trauma among Hindu populations. While not all Mughal rulers pursued such policies, the actions of figures like Aurangzeb have left a lasting imprint on Hindu collective memory.

Resistance figures like Shivaji Maharaj in Maharashtra and Maharana Pratap in Mewar emerged as symbols of cultural resilience during this period. Shivaji, the founder of the Maratha Empire, and Maharana Pratap, who fiercely resisted Mughal expansion, were not just military strategists but also embodiments of a broader struggle to preserve Hindu identity against imperial dominance. Their legacies continue to inspire Hindu nationalist narratives, serving as reminders of a historical struggle for cultural survival and self-determination.

This period of history is complex, with moments of coexistence and conflict. However, the actions of certain rulers and invaders have contributed to a narrative of cultural oppression that continues to shape Hindu nationalist sentiment today. The destruction of temples, the imposition of discriminatory policies, and the resistance of regional heroes are central to this historical memory, underscoring the deep-seated grievances that fuel contemporary political movements.

ಐ

Colonial Impact and Religious Dynamics

The British colonial period introduced another layer of complexity to India's cultural and religious dynamics. Christian missionary activities, coupled with colonial discourse, often portrayed Hindu practices as primitive or backward. This intellectual colonization, which dismissed indigenous traditions, deepened feelings of cultural defensiveness among Hindus.

Post-independence India, under the Congress Party's secular governance led by figures like Jawaharlal Nehru, was perceived by Hindu nationalists as a continuation of cultural marginalization. While the secular model aimed to foster inclusivity, it was often viewed as neglecting or suppressing Hindu cultural identity. This perceived neglect fueled a growing desire among Hindu nationalists to assert their cultural and religious heritage more prominently in the national narrative.

౮

Political Emergence of Hindu Nationalism

The transformation of historical grievances into a cohesive political ideology began with organizations like the Rashtriya Swayamsevak Sangh (RSS), founded in 1925, and later the Bharatiya Janata Party (BJP). These groups framed Hindu nationalism as a movement to reclaim cultural pride and redefine India's national identity in terms of its Hindu majority. Central to this ideology is the concept of Hindutva, which seeks to assert Hindu cultural and political dominance as a response to centuries of perceived marginalization.

The BJP's electoral success, particularly under Narendra Modi's leadership, marks a significant shift in India's political consciousness. Regions with a history of Muslim rule—such as Uttar Pradesh, Rajasthan, Maharashtra, and Karnataka—have shown strong support for the BJP's Hindutva ideology. This support is often rooted in historical memory, where narratives of cultural suppression during periods of Muslim rule, such as the destruction of temples, imposition of discriminatory taxes, and forced conversions, continue to resonate. For many in these regions, the BJP's emphasis on Hindu cultural revival and national pride strikes a chord, offering a sense of historical redress and empowerment.

In contrast, states like Tamil Nadu and Andhra Pradesh, which did not experience prolonged Muslim rule, exhibit different political dynamics. These regions, with their distinct cultural and linguistic identities, often prioritize regionalism over Hindu nationalist narratives. Political parties in these states, such as the Dravida Munnetra

Kazhagam (DMK) in Tamil Nadu and the Yuvajana Sramika Rythu Congress Party (YSRCP) in Andhra Pradesh, focus on local issues, social justice, and regional pride, making it more challenging for the BJP to establish a strong foothold. The absence of a historical narrative of Muslim rule in these areas means that the BJP's Hindutva ideology finds less resonance, highlighting the diversity of India's political and cultural fabric.

This regional variation underscores the profound influence of historical memory on contemporary political preferences. While the BJP's Hindutva ideology has galvanized support in regions with a history of Muslim rule, its appeal remains limited in areas where such historical grievances are absent or overshadowed by other priorities. This dichotomy reflects the complex interplay between history, identity, and politics in shaping India's electoral landscape.

ೞ

Contemporary Political Discourse

The current political discourse under the BJP reflects a desire for what many supporters describe as "true self-rule"—a governance model that explicitly acknowledges and celebrates Hindu cultural identity. This sentiment transcends mere political representation; it represents a psychological and cultural reclamation of space after centuries of perceived suppression.

The BJP's repeated electoral victories underscore the resonance of this narrative among a significant portion of the Hindu population. The party's success is not just electoral but also symbolic, representing a collective assertion of cultural pride and historical identity. Policies such as the construction of the Ram Mandir in Ayodhya, the abrogation of Article 370 in Kashmir, and the promotion of Sanskrit and Hindu traditions reflect this broader cultural agenda.

Conclusion

The rise of Hindu nationalism is more than a political phenomenon; it is a profound expression of cultural memory, historical perception, and collective aspiration. It reflects a desire to reconcile historical grievances with a vision of India that celebrates its Hindu heritage while navigating the complexities of a diverse and pluralistic society.

Understanding Hindu nationalism requires a nuanced engagement with India's historical narratives and contemporary political dynamics. It is a story of identity—complex, multifaceted, and continuously evolving in the world's largest democracy. As India moves forward, the challenge lies in balancing the aspirations of its Hindu majority with the rights and identities of its diverse religious and cultural communities, ensuring that the nation's democratic fabric remains inclusive and resilient.

This revised version improves the flow, adds depth to historical and political analysis, and ensures a balanced tone while maintaining the original article's core message. It also emphasizes the complexity of the issue and the need for nuanced understanding.

IV

Hindu Nationalist Overreach

Since Narendra Modi assumed office as Prime Minister, India has experienced a profound transformation in its sociocultural landscape, marked by the aggressive rise of Hindu nationalism. This ideological shift, rooted in the Hindutva movement, has sought to redefine India's identity, challenging the nation's long-standing traditions of secularism, pluralism, and cultural diversity.

While the government frames these changes as efforts to revive and protect Hindu culture, critics argue that they represent a systematic attempt to impose a homogenized, exclusionary vision of Indian identity, often at the expense of minority communities and regional traditions.

The Rise of Hindutva and Its Sociocultural Impact

Under Modi's leadership, the Bharatiya Janata Party (BJP) and its ideological parent, the Rashtriya Swayamsevak

Sangh (RSS), have pursued policies and social initiatives that prioritize a narrow interpretation of Hindu identity. This agenda has manifested in various forms, from legislative measures to cultural impositions, often alienating religious minorities, linguistic groups, and marginalized communities. The consequences of this overreach are far-reaching, threatening to unravel the pluralistic fabric that has long defined India.

ॐ

Beef Bans: Cultural Imposition and Economic Disruption

One of the most contentious examples of this cultural overreach is the implementation of beef bans across several Indian states. These laws, ostensibly enacted to protect the sentiments of Hindus who revere the cow, disproportionately affect minority communities, particularly Muslims, Christians, and Dalits, for whom beef is an affordable and culturally significant source of protein. In states like Kerala, Goa, and the Northeast, where beef is a dietary staple, these bans have not only disrupted culinary traditions but also jeopardized the livelihoods of farmers, butchers, and small businesses.

Beyond the economic impact, the beef ban symbolizes a broader attempt to impose a singular Hindu cultural narrative on a diverse and multicultural society. By criminalizing a dietary choice deeply embedded in regional cuisines, these policies marginalize communities and exacerbate social tensions. Critics argue that such measures prioritize symbolic gestures over substantive issues like food security and economic inequality.

ॐ

Compulsory Patriotism: Performative Nationalism in Public Spaces

Another manifestation of Hindu nationalist overreach is the enforcement of performative patriotism in public and recreational spaces. Mandatory national anthem screenings in cinemas, accompanied by expectations of standing and visible displays of loyalty, have transformed leisure spaces into arenas of social policing. While patriotism is a cherished value, the compulsion to demonstrate it in specific ways undermines individual autonomy and fosters an environment of fear and conformity.

Such practices not only disrupt the essence of entertainment but also create unnecessary divisions. Even those who consider themselves patriots often find these compulsory displays intrusive and counterproductive, as they conflate genuine love for the country with performative gestures dictated by the state.

ఇ

Linguistic Chauvinism: The Push for Hindi Dominance

The BJP-led government's persistent efforts to promote Hindi as India's dominant national language have reignited historical anxieties about cultural imperialism, particularly in non-Hindi-speaking states like Tamil Nadu, Karnataka, and West Bengal. For these regions, language is not merely a mode of communication but a cornerstone of cultural identity and heritage. The imposition of Hindi risks alienating these communities and exacerbating regional tensions, potentially fueling separatist sentiments.

India's linguistic diversity is one of its greatest strengths, enshrined in the Constitution through the recognition of 22 official languages. By privileging Hindi over regional languages, the government risks undermining this diversity and perpetuating colonial-era hierarchies. A truly inclusive approach would celebrate India's multilingualism rather than impose a homogenized linguistic identity.

ॐ

Moral Policing: Erosion of Personal Freedom

The rise of Hindu nationalist groups has also been accompanied by an increase in moral policing, particularly targeting expressions of personal freedom. Incidents of harassment on Valentine's Day, forced marriages of interfaith couples, and attacks on individuals for allegedly violating "traditional values" reflect a regressive social agenda. These actions, often carried out by self-appointed vigilante groups, seek to control personal choices under the guise of protecting cultural traditions.

Such interventions are particularly harmful to young people, who are increasingly asserting their right to individual autonomy and self-expression. By curtailing these freedoms, Hindu nationalist groups risk alienating an entire generation and fostering a climate of fear and repression.

ॐ

Religious Polarization: Marginalization of Minorities

Perhaps the most alarming aspect of Hindu nationalist overreach is the systematic marginalization of religious minorities, particularly Muslims. Discriminatory policies like the Citizenship Amendment Act (CAA), coupled with inflammatory rhetoric that portrays minorities as outsiders or threats, have deepened communal divisions. The rise in hate speech, mob violence, and targeted attacks against Muslims has created an environment of heightened tension and insecurity.

This polarization not only undermines social harmony but also tarnishes India's global reputation as a pluralistic democracy. By fostering an "us versus them" mentality, the current political discourse risks eroding the trust and solidarity that bind India's diverse communities.

ॐ

Economic and Social Consequences

The cultural and social overreach of Hindu nationalism has significant economic implications. Policies that prioritize ideological goals over practical needs discourage entrepreneurship, stifle innovation, and create an atmosphere of uncertainty. For instance, the beef bans have disrupted supply chains and livelihoods, while moral policing and communal tensions deter investment and tourism.

Moreover, the erosion of individual freedoms and the rise of social anxiety have far-reaching consequences for mental health and social cohesion. A society that prioritizes conformity over creativity and inclusivity risks stagnation and internal conflict.

ॐ

Conclusion: Upholding India's Pluralistic Legacy

The Hindu nationalist agenda under Modi's leadership represents a profound challenge to India's foundational principles of secularism, pluralism, and democracy. By attempting to reshape cultural norms through legislative and social interventions, these policies threaten to undermine the very diversity that has historically been India's greatest strength.

As India moves forward, it is imperative to resist these narrow, exclusionary narratives and recommit to a vision of nationhood that celebrates differences, respects individual choices, and upholds the constitutional values of liberty, equality, and fraternity. Only by embracing its pluralistic legacy can India truly fulfill its potential as a vibrant, inclusive democracy.

V

Modi's Electoral Success: A Victory for Reform or Corporate Interests?

Narendra Modi's electoral dominance has been a defining feature of Indian politics over the past decade. However, the growing disconnect between his government's electoral triumphs and the implementation of meaningful reforms raises critical questions about the true beneficiaries of these victories. While the Bharatiya Janata Party (BJP) continues to secure electoral mandates, mounting evidence suggests that these successes may serve corporate interests—particularly those of the Adani and Ambani conglomerates—more than they advance transformative change for Indian society.

ॐ

The Adani Factor: A Symbiotic Relationship

The Hindenburg Research report in early 2023 exposed the Adani Group's precarious financial position, revealing high leverage and questionable business practices. This revelation underscored a deeper dynamic: the group's meteoric rise appears inextricably tied to government support. Under Modi's administration, the Adani Group has secured a disproportionate share of ports, natural resources, and infrastructure projects, raising concerns about favoritism and crony capitalism.

The group's reliance on government backing creates a mutual dependency. Adani requires state protection to sustain its debt-fueled expansion, while the government seems committed to ensuring the conglomerate's dominance. This relationship transcends typical business-government interactions, suggesting a troubling alignment between political power and corporate interests.

ॐ

Hindutva as a Political Diversion

The BJP's deployment of Hindutva ideology has been a masterstroke in consolidating electoral support. By emphasizing cultural nationalism and religious identity, the party has successfully channeled public sentiment away from pressing socio-economic issues. While this strategy has galvanized the Hindu majority, it has also served as a diversionary tactic, deflecting attention from the government's failure to address systemic challenges.

The BJP's cultural assertiveness has resonated with voters disillusioned by previous governments' perceived minority appeasement policies. However, this focus on identity politics has come at the expense of substantive reforms, leaving critical issues like education, healthcare, and judicial reform unaddressed.

ॐ

The Mirage of Reform

The Modi government has touted several achievements, including infrastructure development, national security enhancements, and banking sector reforms. Yet these accomplishments appear selective and calculated, avoiding the structural changes needed to address India's deep-rooted problems:

- **Education**: The system remains outdated, with inadequate infrastructure and a failure to equip students with modern skills.
- **Healthcare**: Millions still lack access to affordable and quality medical services.
- **Judiciary**: Massive case backlogs and delays undermine justice delivery.
- **Police**: Forces remain underfunded, politicized, and in need of reform.
- **Labor Markets**: Overregulation stifles job creation and economic flexibility.
- **Bureaucracy**: Inefficiency and red tape continue to hamper governance.

These systemic issues persist, suggesting that the government's reforms are more cosmetic than transformative.

ॐ

The Corporate-Political Nexus

A closer look at government decision-making reveals a pattern of policies tailored to benefit select corporate entities. Protectionist measures, preferential resource allocation, and targeted regulatory changes have created an environment where a handful of businesses thrive while competition is stifled. This raises serious questions about the independence of Modi's administration and whether it serves the broader public interest or functions as an instrument of corporate power.

The Adani and Ambani groups, in particular, have benefited from this arrangement, consolidating their dominance across sectors. This corporate-political web not only undermines fair competition but also perpetuates inequality, as smaller businesses and entrepreneurs struggle to compete.

ॐ

The Shadow of Arbitrary Rule Changes: Crony Capitalism and Investor Uncertainty

One of the most concerning aspects of the Modi government's tenure has been the arbitrary changes in rules and regulations that appear to favor select corporate entities, such as the Adani Group, at the expense of fair competition and investor confidence. These sudden policy shifts have created an environment of uncertainty, where businesses fear venturing into sectors dominated by politically connected conglomerates. The government's ability to introduce rules or legislation that disproportionately benefit cronies has deterred investment and stifled innovation, as companies worry about being pushed to the brink of bankruptcy by uneven playing fields.

For instance, in 2020, the government amended the Electricity Act to allow power distribution companies to exit long-term power purchase agreements (PPAs) if they were deemed "burdensome." This move disproportionately benefited Adani Power, which had been struggling with high costs and contractual obligations, while smaller competitors were left vulnerable. Similarly, the abrupt introduction of retrospective taxes in the past—though later repealed—created a climate of distrust among foreign and domestic investors, who feared sudden policy changes could jeopardize their investments.

Such actions not only undermine fair competition but also erode confidence in India's regulatory framework, discouraging long-term investment and economic growth.

The Real Cost of Stagnation
The consequences of this political-corporate nexus are borne by ordinary Indians. While elections are won and stock markets soar, fundamental issues remain unresolved:

- **Education**: The system fails to prepare youth for the job market, exacerbating unemployment.
- **Healthcare**: High medical costs push families into poverty.
- **Justice**: Delays and inefficiencies deny millions access to timely legal recourse.
- **Small Businesses**: They struggle to survive against corporate giants.
- **Innovation**: Protectionist policies stifle creativity and entrepreneurship.

These challenges highlight the gap between electoral rhetoric and governance reality, with the most vulnerable bearing the brunt of inaction.

ॐ

Beyond Electoral Triumphs

The BJP's electoral success, while impressive, appears increasingly hollow when measured against its reform agenda—or lack thereof. The government's overwhelming parliamentary majority, a rare opportunity in Indian politics, has been used more to consolidate power than to drive transformative change. This suggests that electoral victories are not a means to achieve reform but an end in themselves, perpetuating a system that benefits a select few at the expense of the many.

ॐ

The Path Forward

India's development requires more than electoral wins and corporate patronage. Real progress demands:

- **Reducing Corporate Influence:** Breaking the stranglehold of corporate interests on policy-making.
- **Genuine Market Reforms**: Promoting competition and level playing fields for businesses of all sizes.
- **Education and Healthcare Overhaul:** Modernizing these critical sectors to serve all citizens.
- **Judicial and Police Reforms**: Ensuring timely justice and accountable law enforcement.
- **Encouraging Innovation**: Creating an environment that fosters entrepreneurship and technological advancement.

Without these changes, India risks becoming a nation where electoral success masks institutional decay, and corporate interests overshadow national development priorities. The Modi government's reluctance to pursue these reforms, despite its strong mandate, suggests that its priorities lie more in maintaining power and protecting certain business interests than in transforming India's socio-economic landscape.

Conclusion

Narendra Modi's electoral success is undeniable, but its implications for India's future remain contentious. While the BJP has mastered the art of winning elections, its governance record reveals a troubling alignment with corporate interests at the expense of broader societal progress. For India to realize its potential, it must move beyond electoral victories and address the systemic challenges that hinder equitable development. The true measure of success lies not in political dominance but in the transformative reforms that uplift all citizens.

Economic Challenges and Opportunities

This section delves into India's economic contradictions, from the legacy of socialism to the barriers to entrepreneurship and the challenges of escaping the middle-income trap. It also compares India's economic trajectory with China's.

VI

India's Lost Economic Opportunities: A History of Missed Reforms

In the seven decades since independence, India's economic journey resembles a story of paths not taken and opportunities squandered. Despite possessing abundant natural resources, a massive workforce, and entrepreneurial talent, India's economic potential has been repeatedly constrained by policy choices that favored state control over market mechanisms.

From Nehru's embrace of Fabian socialism to the present day, successive governments—regardless of political affiliation—have demonstrated reluctance to fully commit to economic liberalization. This pattern of hesitation has profound implications, as each delayed or abandoned reform represents not just abstract economic inefficiency, but tangible human costs: millions remaining in poverty who might otherwise have enjoyed prosperity, industries that never materialized, and innovations that never took shape.

As India's demographic dividend window gradually narrows toward its projected closure around 2060, the stakes of these policy choices grow ever higher, raising urgent questions about whether the nation can overcome its historical ambivalence toward market economics before this crucial opportunity passes.

The Nehruvian Legacy: Setting the Socialist Path

After gaining independence in 1947, India faced a pivotal choice in its economic direction. Under Jawaharlal Nehru's leadership, the nation embraced Fabian socialism rather than market capitalism. This foundational decision shaped decades of economic policy that followed. Nehru's vision materialized through five-year plans, state-controlled industries, and an elaborate licensing system that came to be known as the "License Raj."

While this approach aimed to ensure equitable development and self-reliance, it inadvertently created a complex bureaucracy that stifled entrepreneurship and economic growth. The absence of competition led to inefficiencies in production, shortages of consumer goods, and ultimately slower economic progress than might have been possible under a more market-oriented system.

The Road Not Taken: Swatantra's Market Vision

During this period, not all political voices supported the socialist approach. Chakravarti Rajagopalachari, affectionately known as Rajaji, founded the Swatantra Party in 1959 as a direct challenge to the Congress Party's socialist policies. The party advocated for free enterprise, minimal government intervention, and market-based solutions to India's economic challenges.

Swatantra gained significant traction initially, becoming the primary opposition in Parliament after the 1967 elections. However, the party's influence waned following Rajaji's death in 1972. Without his charismatic leadership and intellectual heft, the party declined, and with it diminished the most coherent political voice for market liberalization in India. This left socialist ideologies largely unchallenged in mainstream political discourse for the following decades.

౭

Deepening Socialism: The Indira Gandhi Years

Under Indira Gandhi's leadership in the late 1960s and 1970s, India moved even further toward socialism. Her government nationalized major banks in 1969, followed by insurance companies and coal mines. The Foreign Exchange Regulation Act of 1973 further restricted foreign investment, while the Industrial Policy Resolution of 1977 limited the role of large private companies in many sectors.

While these policies were politically popular and aligned with the prevailing "Garibi Hatao" (Remove Poverty) slogan, they further entrenched state control over the economy. The absence of meaningful competition, combined with extensive regulations, continued to constrain India's economic potential. By the 1980s, recognizing some of these limitations, Indira Gandhi began making tentative moves toward economic liberalization, though these efforts remained modest in scope.

ℬ

Crisis and Reform: The 1991 Watershed

It took an economic crisis of unprecedented proportions to finally push India toward fundamental economic reforms. By 1991, the country faced a severe balance of payments crisis, with foreign exchange reserves dwindling to levels that could barely finance three weeks of imports. This crisis forced the hand of P.V. Narasimha Rao's government.

Despite his socialist background, Rao demonstrated remarkable political courage by appointing Manmohan Singh as Finance Minister and supporting the dramatic liberalization measures proposed. The reforms included dismantling the License Raj, reducing trade barriers, welcoming foreign investment, and beginning the process of privatizing state-owned enterprises. These changes unleashed entrepreneurial energies and set India on a path of higher economic growth.

ℬ

Continuation and Caution: 1996-2014

The subsequent governments largely maintained the reform momentum, though at varying paces. Atal Bihari Vajpayee's NDA government (1998-2004) accelerated disinvestment in public sector undertakings and continued liberalizing various sectors of the economy. However, when Manmohan Singh returned as Prime Minister (2004-2014), coalition politics constrained his reform agenda. The UPA government's dependence on left-wing parties for parliamentary support meant that many economic reforms had to be moderated or postponed.

This period saw India's economic growth rate rise substantially from its pre-1991 levels, demonstrating the benefits of the initial reforms. Yet experts increasingly pointed to "second-generation reforms" that remained incomplete – labor laws, agricultural marketing, bureaucratic streamlining, and further privatization – as necessary steps for sustaining high growth rates.

ॐ

Modi Era: Great Expectations, Mixed Delivery

The 2014 election of Narendra Modi with a decisive majority generated widespread expectations of accelerated economic reforms. His campaign slogan of "Minimum Government, Maximum Governance" suggested a commitment to reducing state intervention in the economy and unleashing private enterprise. The initial years saw important initiatives like the Goods and Services Tax and the Insolvency and Bankruptcy Code.

However, the pace and depth of reforms have not matched early expectations. Privatization efforts have been limited, with Air India being a notable exception. The size of government has continued to expand rather than contract. High tax rates, complex regulations, and bureaucratic procedures remain significant obstacles for businesses. Despite having the political mandate that eluded many previous governments, the Modi administration has approached economic liberalization cautiously.

Several factors may explain this approach. Political considerations likely play a role, as reforms often generate short-term disruptions before yielding long-term benefits. The strong influence of the civil service, with its institutional preference for control and regulation, has also shaped policy directions. Additionally, the government has prioritized welfare schemes and infrastructure development over market liberalization as its preferred economic strategy.

శ్రీ

The Demographic Clock: Time Running Out

India's cautious approach to economic reforms takes on greater urgency when viewed against its demographic timeline. The country currently enjoys a "demographic dividend" – a period when working-age individuals constitute a larger proportion of the population than dependents. This advantage provides a window of economic opportunity that demographic projections suggest will last approximately until 2055-2060.

After this period, India's population structure will begin to resemble today's aging economies, with a higher proportion of elderly dependents. This transition will bring different economic challenges. Therefore, the next three decades represent a critical period for implementing reforms that can maximize economic growth and ensure that India achieves higher income levels before its population ages.

శ్రీ

Opposition Politics: Reform Resistance

Compounding the challenge is the nature of opposition politics in India. Rather than advocating for more extensive reforms, opposition parties have frequently resisted liberalization efforts. The farm laws episode of 2020-21 exemplifies this dynamic, where potentially beneficial agricultural market reforms faced such intense opposition that they were ultimately withdrawn. Similar resistance has emerged against labor reforms and attempts to bring lateral entry experts into the bureaucracy.

This pattern creates a political environment where reform initiatives face criticism from multiple directions – from those who believe they go too far and from those who think they don't go far enough. The result is often policy paralysis or watered-down compromises that fail to deliver transformative economic impacts.

৪৩

Conclusion: The Cost of Hesitation

India's economic journey since independence reflects a series of missed opportunities for embracing market-oriented reforms. From the initial choice of Nehruvian socialism to the unfulfilled promise of Modi's "minimum government" vision, political leadership has repeatedly hesitated to fully commit to economic liberalization.

The consequences of these choices are reflected in persistent poverty, lower living standards than might have been achieved, and millions of unrealized aspirations. While the 1991 reforms demonstrated the potential benefits of liberalization, the incomplete nature of India's economic transformation suggests that political considerations continue to outweigh economic imperatives in policy formulation.

As India's demographic window gradually narrows, the urgency for comprehensive reforms increases. The coming decades will determine whether India can overcome its historical reluctance to embrace market principles and unleash its full economic potential, or whether future generations will look back on our current period as yet another chapter in a long history of missed opportunities.

VII

The Economic Cost of State Control: India's Unlearned Lessons

The story of India's economic transformation reveals a tragic tale of squandered potential and lost opportunities. After independence in 1947, India's embrace of Soviet-style central planning didn't just create economic inefficiency – it crushed the dreams and aspirations of entire generations. The infamous "license-permit raj" became more than a bureaucratic nightmare; it represented the systematic destruction of human potential on an unprecedented scale.

The Human Tragedy of Central Planning

The devastating impact of India's socialist policies in the 1970s and 1980s created a lost generation of Indians who saw their prime years wasted in an economic prison of the state's making. Young graduates, armed with degrees but facing a job market strangled by regulations, often spent years in desperate searches for employment. Those fortunate enough to find work faced stagnant wages and limited career prospects. The entrepreneurial spirit that could have transformed the nation was methodically crushed under the weight of over 80 different permits required to start even a small business, each representing an opportunity for corruption and bureaucratic extortion.

Families endured daily humiliations that now seem unconscionable. The wait for a telephone connection could stretch to eight years or more. Those seeking to purchase a scooter might wait up to twelve years, watching their children grow up without the mobility that could have expanded their horizons. The simple act of buying cement required government permission, forcing many to delay or abandon dreams of homeownership. Even basic items like cooking oil and sugar required hours of queuing at government ration shops, time that could have been spent on education or productive work.

❧

China's Economic Miracle: A Story of What Could Have Been

While India imprisoned its citizens in a maze of regulations, China's pragmatic turn to market economics in 1978 unleashed an economic miracle that would redefine global power dynamics. The contrast couldn't be more stark: as Indian entrepreneurs struggled to navigate hundreds of permits and bribes, their Chinese counterparts were building factories and creating millions of jobs. Within just two decades, China had lifted over 800 million people out of poverty – the largest such achievement in human history. The average Chinese citizen saw their income multiply several times over, while their Indian counterparts remained trapped in chronic poverty.

What makes this contrast particularly painful is that both nations started from similar points of economic development in the 1950s. China's transformation from an impoverished nation to the world's second-largest economy stands as a damning indictment of India's policy choices. While Indian bureaucrats debated the color of ink required on permit applications, China was building world-class infrastructure and becoming the world's manufacturing hub.

ॐ

The 1991 Watershed: A Breath of Freedom After Decades of Suffocation

The 1991 reforms under Prime Minister Narasimha Rao and Finance Minister Manmohan Singh came not a moment too soon for a suffocating nation. For the first time in decades, Indians could dream of starting a business without navigating an endless maze of permits. The dismantling of industrial licensing felt like the breaking of chains that had bound generations. Young entrepreneurs, who had watched their parents' generation waste away in the stranglehold of bureaucracy, could finally dare to dream bigger.

The reforms represented more than economic policy changes – they were a liberation of the Indian spirit. Families who had spent decades accepting shortages and rationing as a way of life suddenly found themselves with choices. The end of the "quota system" meant that merit and market forces, not political connections, would determine success. A new generation of Indians could finally compete on the global stage, unleashing decades of pent-up creative and entrepreneurial energy.

ॐ

Contemporary Concerns: The Shadow of the Past Looms Again

Yet today, we witness a disturbing echo of those dark decades. The "Atmanirbhar Bharat" initiative, while wrapped in the rhetoric of self-reliance, carries haunting similarities to the protectionist policies that once imprisoned India's economic potential. The growing complexity of regulations in sectors like e-commerce and digital services threatens to create a new generation of bureaucratic gatekeepers, reminiscent of the officials who once decided which industries could produce what and how much.

For those who lived through the pre-1991 era, these trends trigger painful memories of a time when every business decision required a bureaucrat's stamp, when innovation was stifled by red tape, and when corruption was not just common but necessary for survival. The younger generation, having never experienced the soul-crushing weight of the license-permit raj, risks underestimating the dangers of returning to state control.

ॐ

The Cost of Policy Amnesia: A Nation at Risk of Repeating Its Mistakes

The human cost of forgetting these lessons would be catastrophic. We need only look at the lives damaged by the pre-1991 policies: the brilliant minds who never got to build their dreams, the innovations that died in government offices, the countless hours wasted in permit queues that could have been spent creating value. Meanwhile, China's continued economic rise serves as a constant reminder of the path not taken. While India debated protectionist policies, China opened its markets wider, becoming the world's factory and lifting hundreds of millions more into the middle class.

ॐ

Production-Linked Incentives: Echoes of Failed Industrial Policy

The current PLI schemes, despite their modern packaging, risk recreating the same byzantine system that once paralyzed Indian industry. By allowing bureaucrats to pick winners and losers, we risk returning to an era where political connections matter more than efficiency or innovation. The same mindset that once required Indians to wait years for a telephone connection now threatens to determine which industries deserve government support and which don't.

ॐ

The Way Forward: Learning from Past Suffering

The path to sustained prosperity requires remembering the human toll of excessive state control. India must:

- Strip away the layers of regulation that still bind entrepreneurial energy
- Eliminate the discretionary powers that breed corruption
- Embrace competition as the driver of innovation and growth
- Create clear, simple rules that apply equally to all

- Focus state resources on education and infrastructure while letting private enterprise drive growth

ॐ

Conclusion: A Choice Between Freedom and Chains

The cost of ignoring history's lessons goes far beyond immediate economic indicators. Pre-1991 policies led to a lost generation of Indian potential, and the current trend towards state control risks compromising future opportunities. In an increasingly competitive global economy, India cannot afford to repeat the economic mistakes of the past.

India's economic history clearly shows that prosperity comes from economic freedom, competition, and clear rules, not state control or bureaucratic discretion. At this crucial juncture, policymakers must choose to learn from history or risk repeating it. The stakes - the economic opportunities and aspirations of millions of Indians - could not be higher.

India stands at a crossroads, with the ghosts of its socialist past beckoning it backward. The choice is stark: continue the path of economic freedom that has created millions of opportunities since 1991, or risk returning to the dark days of state control. The stakes are not just economic indicators but the dreams and aspirations of millions of young Indians. We must not condemn another generation to the frustration and hopelessness of the pre-1991 era. The time has come to fully embrace the lessons of history and choose the path of economic freedom, not just for growth statistics, but for the human potential that awaits liberation.

VIII

The Socialist Hangover: How Non-Market Participants Drive India's Economic Discourse

The persistent influence of socialist thinking in India's economic discourse presents a fascinating paradox: many of its most vocal proponents have never directly participated in wealth creation. This disconnect between theoretical knowledge and practical experience continues to shape India's economic policies and institutional frameworks in significant ways and potentially hinders its transition to a more market-oriented economy.

ॐ

The Academic-Bureaucratic Echo Chamber

At the heart of this phenomenon lies a self-reinforcing system where academics and bureaucrats, despite their limited exposure to market forces, wield considerable influence over economic policy. University professors, ensconced in government-funded institutions, often advocate for socialist policies without having experienced the challenges of running a business or competing in the market. Similarly, civil servants typically move directly from academic institutions to government service, spending their careers managing and redistributing wealth rather than creating it.

This was particularly evident during the planning commission era, where bureaucrats designed elaborate five-year plans that directed India's economic trajectory. The results were reflected in the nation's underwhelming economic performance during the pre-1991 period, commonly referred to as the "Hindu rate of growth."

ॐ

The Trade Union Paradox

Trade unions represent another dimension of this disconnect. Many union leaders, particularly in the public sector, operate from a theoretical understanding of market dynamics without direct experience in competitive industries. Despite this limitation, they continue to exert substantial influence over labor policies and industrial relations. Their positions often reflect ideological preferences rather than practical considerations about job creation and economic growth.

ॐ

The State Enterprise Conundrum

The state-owned enterprise sector perfectly illustrates this paradox. Many advocates for maintaining large public sector undertakings have spent their entire careers in protected environments, shielded from market pressures. Their resistance to privatization often stems from limited understanding of the efficiency demands and innovation pressures faced by private enterprises in competitive markets.

ॐ

Media and Policy Analysis: Theory Without Practice

This disconnect extends to media commentators and policy analysts who, while prolific in their economic commentary, often lack practical experience in wealth creation. Their narratives tend to romanticize state control while underestimating the efficiency gains that market competition can deliver. This theoretical approach to economic analysis often results in policies that fail to address the real-world challenges faced by businesses and entrepreneurs.

ॐ

The China Contrast

The contrast with China's economic transformation is instructive. Post-1978, under Deng Xiaoping's leadership, China embraced a pragmatic approach to market reforms, prioritizing practical outcomes over ideological purity. This approach, embodied in Deng's famous cat analogy, helped transform China into the world's second-largest economy. Meanwhile, India's economic liberals faced persistent resistance from some economists termed the "permanent establishment" – a coalition deeply invested in maintaining socialist structures.

$$\text{ɞ}$$

Real-World Consequences

This theory-practice disconnect has tangible implications for India's economic development. Policy discussions often prioritize theoretical constructs over practical business realities, resulting in regulations that reflect an academic understanding of markets rather than the actual needs of entrepreneurs. Labor laws, in particular, frequently embody idealistic notions that can inadvertently impede economic growth and job creation.

$$\text{ɞ}$$

The Path Forward

Bridging this gap between theory and practice requires a more balanced approach to economic policymaking. While academic expertise remains valuable, it needs to be complemented by insights from those with direct experience in wealth creation. This could involve including more business practitioners in policy consultations, exposing bureaucrats to private sector assignments, and giving greater weight to empirical evidence over theoretical constructs.

$$\text{ɞ}$$

Conclusion

India's economic future hinges on successfully reconciling theoretical knowledge with practical market experience. As the country seeks to accelerate its development, it needs voices that understand both economic frameworks and the real-world challenges of creating wealth in competitive markets. Only through this synthesis can India fully embrace the market reforms necessary to achieve its economic potential.

The persistence of socialist thinking among those removed from wealth creation represents more than just an academic curiosity – it reflects a deeper institutional challenge that India must address to advance its economic agenda. The path forward requires not just policy changes but a fundamental shift in how economic expertise is defined and valued in policy circles. This transition, while challenging, is essential for India to fully capitalize on its economic potential and create sustainable prosperity for its growing population.

IX

Entrenched Interests vs. Common Prosperity

India's political landscape reveals a troubling pattern that has persisted across decades and governments of different ideologies. Political power often functions as a revolving door where different entrenched groups take turns governing, not to implement transformative policies, but to protect their own established interests. This cyclical pattern has created a governance approach where the primary objective becomes securing votes rather than enabling nationwide economic upliftment.

What we observe is a political ecosystem that thrives on short-term thinking. Instead of crafting comprehensive policies that might take years or decades to fully materialize, political actors prefer immediate gratification through voter appeasement schemes. The deep-rooted problem is that these temporary benefits—subsidies, loan waivers, and various forms of direct cash transfers—may provide momentary relief but fail to address structural economic barriers that keep millions trapped in cycles of poverty.

The Missing Market Economy Vision

Perhaps the most telling symptom of this entrenchment problem is the absence of a strong political movement advocating for a true market economy in India. Despite economic liberalization in 1991, which partially opened India's economy, the country still operates under layers of regulations that stifle entrepreneurial energy. No major political party has championed comprehensive economic liberalization—reducing excessive regulations, simplifying tax structures, eliminating bureaucratic hurdles, and truly creating an environment where businesses can thrive without political patronage.

This absence isn't accidental. A genuinely open market economy would threaten the very power structures that benefit from the current system of permits, licenses, and discretionary approvals. The persistence of these regulatory barriers ensures that economic success often depends more on political connections than on innovation or efficiency. The result is an economy where established players are protected while new entrants face substantial barriers.

The Entrepreneurship Bottleneck

For ordinary citizens with entrepreneurial ambitions, the path is fraught with obstacles. Starting and operating a business in India involves navigating complex regulatory frameworks that can vary across states, municipalities, and even departments within the same government. The World Bank's Ease of Doing Business rankings have shown improvement for India in recent years, but the ground reality for small and medium enterprises remains challenging.

Consider the typical journey of an entrepreneur in India: obtaining multiple licenses, seeking approvals from various government departments, complying with labor regulations designed for larger enterprises, managing complex tax requirements, and often encountering demands for informal payments to expedite processes. Each step presents an opportunity for delay, additional cost, or even project abandonment. This regulatory maze effectively functions as a filter that allows only the most persistent or well-connected entrepreneurs to succeed.

੮ఌ

The Flight to Unproductive Assets
When productive enterprise becomes excessively difficult, capital naturally flows toward safer, if less productive, investments. This explains the traditional Indian preference for gold and real estate as stores of value. These assets provide security and appreciation without the operational headaches of running a business.

However, this capital allocation pattern has significant economic consequences. Gold, while culturally important and individually rational as a store of value, represents static wealth that could otherwise fund productive ventures creating jobs and innovations. Similarly, real estate investment often becomes speculative rather than development-focused, driving up prices without necessarily improving infrastructure or living standards.

The irony is that India possesses abundant capital—household savings rates remain relatively high by global standards—but these resources aren't efficiently channeled toward productive enterprise. The financial system, still dominated by public sector banks with their own inefficiencies and risk aversion, further compounds this problem by preferentially lending to established businesses rather than new ventures.

The Elusive Industrial Revolution

The cumulative effect of these factors explains why India has struggled to develop a robust manufacturing sector. While services, particularly information technology, have thrived in certain enclaves that managed to partially escape the regulatory burden, manufacturing requires more intensive capital investment, infrastructure support, and regulatory predictability.

Manufacturing also requires policy continuity across political administrations—factories aren't built and supply chains aren't established based on five-year electoral cycles. The absence of this continuity, combined with infrastructure deficiencies, regulatory complexity, and labor market rigidities, has prevented India from becoming a manufacturing powerhouse despite its demographic advantages of a young, growing workforce.

What's particularly concerning is that this isn't merely a historical observation about missing the 18th-century Industrial Revolution—India continues to miss opportunities to establish itself as a manufacturing hub even as global supply chains reconfigure and countries seek alternatives to existing production centers. The window for labor-intensive manufacturing as a development pathway may be narrowing with increasing automation, making the missed opportunities even more costly.

Breaking the Cycle: Possible Pathways

Breaking free from this entrenched pattern requires fundamental reforms that seem politically difficult precisely because they threaten established interests. However, several potential pathways could help India transition toward a more dynamic, opportunity-rich economy:

First, regulatory simplification must be pursued not just as a slogan but as a comprehensive program touching every aspect of business operation. This means not merely digitizing existing processes but fundamentally questioning whether many regulations serve any public purpose beyond creating opportunities for rent-seeking.

Second, decentralization of economic governance could allow states to experiment with policy innovations, creating competitive federalism that rewards pro-growth policies. States that successfully create entrepreneurial ecosystems could demonstrate viable alternatives to the status quo.

Third, educational reforms focused on practical skills, problem-solving, and entrepreneurial thinking could gradually shift cultural attitudes toward risk-taking and business creation. The current educational system, with its emphasis on credentials over capabilities, reinforces existing patterns of seeking secure employment rather than creating new ventures.

Finally, civil society organizations and independent media have crucial roles in highlighting the costs of regulatory barriers and advocating for reforms that benefit broader segments of society rather than entrenched interests.

ॐ

Conclusion: The Urgency of Economic Democratization

The challenge India faces isn't simply about economic growth as an abstract number—it's about whether that growth creates broad-based opportunities or simply enriches those already connected to power. True economic development requires democratizing opportunity, ensuring that success depends more on innovation, effort, and skill than on navigating Byzantine regulations or leveraging political connections.

The stakes couldn't be higher. India's demographic dividend—the large youth population entering the workforce—represents either an unprecedented opportunity or a potential source of instability if sufficient productive employment isn't created. The country's political leadership, regardless of party affiliation, must recognize that protecting entrenched economic interests ultimately threatens India's social cohesion and long-term stability.

What India needs is not incremental change but a fundamental reimagining of the relationship between state and market—one that empowers ordinary citizens to pursue their economic aspirations without unnecessary barriers. Only then can India fulfill its potential as not just a large economy but a truly prosperous and opportunity-rich society.

X

The Credit Barrier: Unlocking Entrepreneurial Potential

India's entrepreneurial landscape stands at a critical juncture where immense potential meets systemic obstacles. At the heart of this challenge lies the traditional collateral-based lending system that effectively blocks millions of ambitious young Indians from pursuing their entrepreneurial dreams. This barrier not only stifles individual aspirations but also significantly hampers India's economic growth potential and innovation ecosystem.

The Current System's Fundamental Flaw

The current lending system in India operates on a fundamentally flawed premise: that past wealth accumulation, primarily in the form of property and assets, should determine future entrepreneurial opportunities. This creates a paradoxical situation where young innovators with promising ideas must either wait years to build collateral or abandon their entrepreneurial ambitions altogether. The result is a massive loss of entrepreneurial energy that could otherwise drive economic growth, job creation, and innovation.

☙

Limitations of Government Initiatives

The government's Mudra loan scheme, while well-intentioned, has proven insufficient to address this systemic challenge. Government initiatives, by their nature, are constrained by bureaucratic processes, limited resources, and the need to maintain conservative lending practices with public funds. The real solution must emerge from the private banking sector, which has the capacity, expertise, and financial resources to revolutionize entrepreneurial lending.

☙

Alternative Assessment Models

Private banks must pioneer new models of credit assessment that move beyond traditional collateral. These models should evaluate entrepreneurs based on a holistic set of criteria, including:

- **Business Plan Viability**: The innovation potential and feasibility of the proposed venture.

- **Educational Background and Skills**: The entrepreneur's academic qualifications and relevant expertise.
- **Market Analysis**: The growth potential and market demand for the proposed product or service.
- **Professional Track Record**: Past achievements and professional experience.
- **Character Assessment**: The entrepreneur's commitment to the venture, their integrity and resilience.

ॐ

Global Success Stories

Several global examples demonstrate the feasibility of such alternative lending approaches. Microfinance institutions have successfully used group lending and social collateral models. Modern fintech companies employ sophisticated algorithms to assess creditworthiness based on alternative data points. These innovations prove that moving beyond traditional collateral-based lending is not only possible but can be profitable.

ॐ

The High Cost of Inaction

The cost of maintaining the status quo is enormous. When entrepreneurship becomes a privilege reserved for those with inherited wealth or accumulated assets, society loses out on countless innovative solutions to pressing problems. A young engineer might have the perfect solution to urban waste management, or a passionate educator might have an innovative approach to rural education, but without access to credit, these solutions remain unrealized dreams.

ॐ

Generational Impact

The generational impact of this credit barrier is particularly concerning. In a country where a significant portion of the population is young, forcing potential entrepreneurs to wait for years or generations to accumulate collateral means losing the demographic dividend that could drive India's economic growth. The energy, creativity, and risk-taking appetite characteristic of youth are valuable resources that should be leveraged, not suppressed.

଼

Solutions and Opportunities for Private Banks

Private banks have a unique opportunity to lead the charge in transforming India's entrepreneurial lending landscape. By developing innovative lending products tailored for entrepreneurs, they can tap into a vast market of ambitious individuals while contributing to national economic growth. Potential solutions include:

- **Staged Lending**: Providing funds in stages based on the achievement of specific milestones.
- **Revenue-Based Financing**: Offering loans with repayment terms tied to the venture's revenue.
- **Hybrid Models**: Combining traditional collateral with alternative assessment methods.
- **Partnerships with Incubators:** Collaborating with incubators and accelerators for better risk assessment.
- **Technology Integration:** Leveraging technology for continuous monitoring and support.

଼

The Path Forward: A Paradigm Shift

The transformation of India's entrepreneurial lending landscape requires a shift in mindset from both lenders and regulators. Banks need to move from a security-first approach to a potential-first approach, while regulators must create frameworks that encourage innovation in lending while maintaining system stability.

Success in this transformation could create a virtuous cycle. As more entrepreneurs gain access to credit and build successful businesses, they create case studies and precedents that make banks more confident in lending to future entrepreneurs. This could lead to a self-sustaining ecosystem where entrepreneurial success breeds more entrepreneurial opportunities.

ॐ

Conclusion: Unleashing India's Entrepreneurial Potential

For India to realize its ambition of becoming a global economic powerhouse, unleashing its entrepreneurial potential is crucial. The current collateral-based system effectively locks out a vast pool of talent and innovation, creating an artificial barrier to economic growth and social progress. While government initiatives like Mudra loans play a role, the real solution lies in private sector innovation in credit assessment and lending.

The time has come for India's private banking sector to step up and create new pathways for entrepreneurial funding. By looking beyond traditional collateral and developing sophisticated methods to assess and support entrepreneurs, banks can unlock tremendous value – both for themselves and for the nation. The future of India's entrepreneurial ecosystem depends on making this crucial transition from asset-based lending to potential-based lending.

XI

Economic Accessibility and Crime Reduction

Social and economic inclusivity plays a vital role in crime prevention, particularly in developing nations like India where significant portions of the population still struggle with poverty and unemployment. When society creates high barriers to legitimate economic participation, it inadvertently pushes vulnerable individuals toward criminal activities.

The relationship between economic opportunity and crime has been evident throughout India's economic history. Prior to the 1991 economic liberalization, the country's restrictive economic policies and limited job opportunities left vast segments of the population unemployed. This situation was particularly dire for those without property or formal education, as the conventional paths to earning a legitimate income were effectively closed to them. When individuals find themselves unable to meet their basic needs through legal means, some resort to crimes like theft and dacoity not out of moral failure, but out of desperate necessity.

Social Barriers and Caste Discrimination

The challenge is further complicated by social barriers, particularly in rural India where caste-based discrimination continues to impact economic mobility. When certain groups face social ostracization, their ability to participate in the local economy is severely restricted. This social exclusion often creates a self-perpetuating cycle where limited economic opportunities reinforce social marginalization, pushing individuals toward illegal activities as a means of survival.

Small-Scale Entrepreneurship as a Solution

The solution lies in creating accessible entry points to legitimate economic activity. Small-scale entrepreneurship, such as street vending, represents one of the most viable paths for economically disadvantaged individuals to enter the formal economy. When someone can freely set up a small business selling items like peanuts or snacks in high-traffic areas, they gain not just an income stream but also a foothold in legitimate society. This initial entry point, however modest, can serve as the foundation for future growth and expansion.

Regulatory Hurdles and Their Impact

However, this potential path out of poverty is often blocked by excessive regulatory requirements and enforcement. When street vendors face harassment from local authorities, need to navigate complex licensing procedures, or must pay bribes to operate, the barrier to entry becomes insurmountable for those with minimal resources. These regulatory hurdles, while potentially well-intentioned, can effectively criminalize poverty by making it impossible for the poorest members of society to participate in legitimate economic activities.

ॐ

Policy Recommendations

The policy implications are clear: governments should prioritize creating an environment where small-scale entrepreneurship can flourish without excessive regulation. This doesn't mean eliminating all oversight, but rather adopting a more nuanced approach that recognizes the role of informal economic activities in poverty alleviation and crime prevention. Basic health and safety standards can be maintained without imposing burdensome regulatory requirements that effectively exclude the poor from participating in the economy.

Several practical steps can be taken to implement this approach:

1. Municipalities should establish designated zones where small-scale vendors can operate without formal licenses or with minimal regulatory requirements. These zones could be located in areas with high foot traffic, such as near public transportation hubs, parks, and tourist destinations.

2. Law enforcement approaches should be reformed to focus on supporting rather than hindering small-scale entrepreneurs. Instead of viewing street vendors as nuisances to be removed, police should be trained to recognize their role in preventing crime through economic opportunity.

3. Simplified registration systems could be implemented for small businesses, with minimal paperwork and fees. This would allow entrepreneurs to gradually transition from informal to formal operations as their businesses grow, without facing prohibitive initial barriers.

Broader Economic Benefits

The benefits of such an approach extend beyond crime prevention. When individuals can freely participate in legitimate economic activities, they not only support themselves but also contribute to the local economy. Their success can inspire others in their community, creating positive role models and demonstrating viable alternatives to criminal activity.

Furthermore, this approach aligns with India's broader economic development goals. By making it easier for people to start small businesses, the country can harness its entrepreneurial potential and create more inclusive economic growth. This is particularly important given India's large youth population and the ongoing challenge of creating sufficient formal sector jobs.

Conclusion

In conclusion, the relationship between economic accessibility and crime prevention cannot be overlooked. When society makes it difficult for individuals to participate in legitimate economic activities, it inadvertently creates conditions that foster criminal behavior. By removing unnecessary barriers to entry for small-scale entrepreneurship and creating more inclusive economic opportunities, India can address both poverty and crime prevention simultaneously. The key lies in recognizing that economic participation is not just about creating wealth, but about providing individuals with dignified alternatives to criminal activity. As India continues its economic development journey, ensuring easy entry into legitimate economic activities should be a central component of both its crime prevention and poverty reduction strategies.

XII

Avoiding the Lower Middle-Income Trap

India, once hailed as the next global economic powerhouse, is now facing a critical juncture in its development trajectory. With a per capita GDP of around $2,700, the country risks being trapped in the lower middle-income category, unable to achieve the high-income status that its vast population and potential demand. Slowing economic growth, stalled reforms, an outdated education system, and a rapidly aging population are all contributing to this precarious situation. If India is to avoid this trap, it must act decisively to implement transformative reforms and reignite its growth engine.

Slowing Growth and Stalled Reforms

India's economic growth, which once soared at 8-9% annually, has now plateaued at 5-6%. This slowdown is particularly concerning given the country's need to create jobs for its young and growing population. While the Modi government has made some strides in improving infrastructure and implementing initiatives like the Goods and Services Tax (GST), it has largely stalled on big-ticket reforms. Key areas such as labor laws, privatization of public sector enterprises, banking sector reforms, and reducing bureaucratic red tape remain untouched or have seen only incremental progress.

The lack of bold reforms has stifled private investment and entrepreneurship, which are critical for sustained economic growth. India's regulatory environment remains cumbersome, discouraging both domestic and foreign investors. Without significant deregulation and a push toward privatization, the economy is unlikely to break free from its current stagnation.

❧

The Education Crisis: A Ticking Time Bomb

India's education system is another major bottleneck. Despite producing millions of graduates annually, a significant proportion are deemed unemployable due to a lack of practical skills. The system continues to rely heavily on rote learning and memorization, rather than fostering critical thinking, problem-solving, and hands-on learning. This has created a mismatch between the skills of the workforce and the demands of the modern economy.

The rise of Artificial Intelligence (AI) and automation further exacerbates this challenge. Many knowledge-sector jobs, which have been a ladder for social mobility for India's middle class over the past three decades, are now at risk of being automated. If India fails to overhaul its education system to focus on creativity, innovation, and adaptability, it risks losing its competitive edge in the global economy.

ॐ

Losing the Demographic Dividend

India's demographic dividend, once seen as its greatest asset, is also under threat. While the country still has a relatively young population, the window of opportunity is closing as the population begins to age. By 2050, India is projected to have over 300 million people aged 60 and above. This demographic shift poses a dual challenge: the need to create jobs for the youth while simultaneously preparing for the healthcare and social security needs of an aging population.

The risk of "growing old before getting rich" is very real. Countries like China and South Korea leveraged their demographic dividends to achieve rapid economic growth and transition to high-income status. India, however, risks squandering this opportunity if it does not act swiftly to create jobs, improve productivity, and invest in human capital.

ॐ

The Path Forward: Bold Reforms and Sustained Growth

To avoid the lower middle-income trap, India must embark on a path of bold and comprehensive reforms. Here are some key areas that require immediate attention:

- **Economic Reforms:** The government must prioritize labor law reforms to make hiring and firing easier, thereby encouraging job creation. Privatization of inefficient public sector enterprises and banks should be accelerated to reduce the fiscal burden and improve efficiency. Reducing bureaucratic red tape and arbitrary regulations will foster a more business-friendly environment.

- **Education Overhaul**: India needs to shift from an examination-centric system to one that emphasizes critical thinking, problem-solving, and practical skills. Vocational training and STEM education should be prioritized to align with the demands of the modern economy. Public-private partnerships can play a crucial role in bridging the skill gap.

- **Healthcare and Social Security**: With an aging population, India must invest in healthcare infrastructure and social security systems. Universal healthcare coverage and pension schemes will be essential to support the elderly and reduce the burden on families.

- **Judicial and Police Reforms**: A robust and efficient judiciary and police system are critical for maintaining law and order and ensuring a conducive environment for business. Reforms in these areas will enhance investor confidence and improve the ease of doing business.

- **Sustained High Growth**: To achieve high-income status, India needs to grow at 9-10% annually for a sustained period. This will require not only economic reforms but also investments in infrastructure, technology, and innovation.

स

Conclusion

India stands at a critical crossroads. The choices it makes today will determine whether it can break free from the lower middle-income trap and achieve its full potential. While the challenges are daunting, they are not insurmountable. With bold reforms, a focus on education and skill development, and a commitment to sustained high growth, India can still chart a path toward prosperity. The time to act is now, before the window of opportunity closes for good.

XIII

Bridging the Gap with China

In the complex landscape of Asian geopolitics, India faces a critical challenge in countering China's growing influence. The economic disparity between these two Asian giants has significant implications for regional power dynamics, military capabilities, and strategic autonomy. With India's economy currently standing at approximately one-fourth of China's size, the need for transformative economic reforms has never been more urgent.

The Current Economic Disparity

The stark contrast between India and China's economic trajectories becomes evident when examining their post-independence journeys. While China embarked on revolutionary economic reforms under Deng Xiaoping in 1978, embracing market principles while maintaining state control, India's economic liberalization came later in 1991.

This head start, combined with China's focused approach to manufacturing, infrastructure development, and export-oriented growth, has resulted in a significant economic gap between the two nations.

Today, China's economy dwarfs India's, with implications extending far beyond GDP figures. This disparity affects everything from military modernization capabilities to diplomatic leverage in international forums. The gap is particularly concerning given China's increasingly assertive stance in the Indo-Pacific region and along the disputed border areas.

Military and Strategic Implications

The economic gap directly translates into military capabilities. China's larger economy allows it to allocate substantially more resources to military modernization, research and development, and force projection capabilities. While India maintains a professional and capable military, the resource constraints imposed by a smaller economy limit its ability to match China's military investments, particularly in emerging technologies like artificial intelligence, hypersonic weapons, and space capabilities.

Furthermore, economic strength provides China with significant diplomatic leverage through initiatives like the Belt and Road Initiative (BRI), which India has consciously stayed away from. This economic diplomacy allows China to build strategic relationships that could potentially isolate India in its own neighborhood.

The Reform Imperative

To address this strategic vulnerability, India must unleash its economic potential through comprehensive reforms. The reference to "animal spirits" in the economy, a term popularized by economist John Maynard Keynes, points to the need for policies that boost business confidence and entrepreneurial activity. Several key areas require immediate attention:

First, labor reforms must balance worker protection with market flexibility. India's complex labor laws often discourage formal sector employment and limit manufacturing scale. Second, land acquisition reforms are crucial for infrastructure development and industrial growth. Third, the financial sector needs strengthening to improve credit flow to productive sectors of the economy.

ॐ

Learning from China's Reform Experience

China's post-1978 reforms under Deng Xiaoping offer valuable lessons. The gradual opening of the economy, focus on special economic zones, emphasis on export-oriented manufacturing, and massive infrastructure investment created the foundation for China's economic miracle. While India need not replicate China's model exactly, given its democratic setup and different institutional framework, certain principles remain relevant.

These include the need for policy consistency, focus on comparative advantages, investment in human capital, and creation of an enabling environment for both domestic and foreign investment. India's demographic dividend, which China is losing due to its aging population, could be a significant advantage if properly leveraged.

ॐ

The Path Forward

To move from a low middle-income to a middle-income country and achieve at least half of China's GDP, India needs to maintain sustained high growth rates while addressing structural challenges. This requires a multi-pronged approach:

- Improving ease of doing business must remain a priority, reducing bureaucratic hurdles and compliance costs. Infrastructure development, both physical and digital, needs acceleration to reduce logistics costs and improve competitiveness. Education and skill development require significant investment to prepare the workforce for future opportunities.
- The development of robust manufacturing capabilities is crucial, particularly in strategic sectors. This would not only generate employment but also reduce strategic vulnerabilities in global supply chains, as highlighted by recent global events.

ಉ

Conclusion

The imperative for India to accelerate its economic growth is not merely an economic challenge but a strategic necessity. The current economic gap with China creates vulnerabilities that extend beyond trade imbalances to core national security concerns. While the task of catching up with China's economy is daunting, India has significant advantages including a young population, democratic institutions, and a vibrant entrepreneurial culture.

The key lies in implementing bold reforms that release the economy's potential while maintaining social cohesion and environmental sustainability. As China's experience shows, transformative economic growth is possible with the right policies and determined implementation. For India, the choice is clear: either undertake comprehensive reforms to accelerate growth or risk falling further behind in the strategic competition with China. The consequences of maintaining the status quo could impact not just India's economic future but its ability to maintain strategic autonomy and protect its interests in an increasingly complex geopolitical environment.

Social Fractures and Identity Politics

This section addresses India's deep social divides, including religious, caste, and regional disparities. It also examines the rise of the middle class and its impact on collective consciousness.

XIV

Economic Marginalization of Muslims in Contemporary India

The economic marginalization of India's Muslim minority has become an increasingly discussed phenomenon, with various policies and social dynamics contributing to growing economic segregation and reduced opportunities. This complex issue involves multiple interconnected factors ranging from direct policy impacts to indirect social and economic effects.

Economic Restrictions and Their Impact

The restrictions on cattle slaughter and beef trade have had significant economic ramifications for Muslim communities traditionally involved in these sectors. The leather industry, which historically provided employment to many Muslims, has faced disruptions. Traditional butcher shops and meat processing units, often family-run businesses passed down through generations, have been forced to close or significantly alter their operations. These restrictions have affected not just business owners but entire supply chains, including transporters, workers, and allied industries.

The impact extends beyond just the meat industry. Food service establishments owned by Muslims have faced challenges due to misinformation campaigns and social media rumors. The spread of unsubstantiated claims about food contamination has led to boycotts and reduced patronage of Muslim-owned establishments, affecting their economic viability. Some restaurant owners have reported having to hide their religious identity or rebrand their businesses to survive.

&

Housing and Spatial Segregation

Economic pressures have contributed to increased spatial segregation in urban areas. Muslims face difficulties in renting or purchasing properties in certain neighborhoods, leading to concentrated settlement patterns. This "ghettoisation" process creates a cycle where:

1. Limited housing options force communities into specific areas
2. Property values in these areas often remain depressed

3. Reduced property values limit wealth accumulation through real estate
4. Concentration in specific areas can limit access to broader economic opportunities

The phenomenon has been particularly visible in major urban centers where housing discrimination, both subtle and overt, has led to the formation of distinct Muslim-majority localities. These areas often suffer from inadequate infrastructure and reduced access to public services.

ॐ

Access to Financial Services

Reports indicate disparities in access to formal banking and financial services. Studies have shown lower approval rates for business loans and mortgages for Muslim applicants. This limited access to formal credit often forces reliance on informal lending networks, which typically charge higher interest rates and offer less favorable terms. The resulting higher cost of capital creates additional barriers to business expansion and economic mobility.

Small businesses, particularly those owned by Muslims, face challenges in securing working capital and expansion loans. This financial exclusion has become more pronounced in recent years, affecting everything from street vendors to medium-sized enterprises.

ॐ

Educational and Employment Opportunities

Economic marginalization has created ripple effects in education and employment. Reduced household incomes affect families' ability to invest in education, particularly higher education. This impact on educational attainment can perpetuate economic disparities across generations.

In the employment sector, there are reports of discrimination in hiring practices, particularly in the private sector. This has led many qualified professionals to either:

- Seek employment opportunities abroad
- Accept positions below their qualification level
- Start small businesses in their community areas

The resulting brain drain affects not just individual families but the broader economic potential of the community.

‮಄‬

Impact on Women's Economic Participation

Muslim women face compound challenges due to both gender and religious identity. Traditional industries that employed Muslim women have seen disruptions, while access to new economic opportunities remains limited. This has affected female labor force participation rates and household income levels in Muslim families.

‮಄‬

Community Response and Adaptation

In response to these challenges, Muslim communities have developed various coping strategies:

- Formation of informal business networks and support systems
- Development of community-based financial solutions
- Focus on education and skill development

- Diversification into new business sectors

Some communities have successfully adapted by moving into emerging sectors like technology and digital services, which are less susceptible to traditional forms of discrimination.

ℬ

Long-term Economic Implications

The ongoing economic marginalization raises concerns about long-term impacts on social mobility and economic integration. The concentration of communities in specific areas, combined with reduced economic opportunities, risks creating isolated economic ecosystems with limited growth potential.

This segregation can lead to:

- Reduced economic diversity within communities
- Limited exposure to broader market opportunities
- Decreased social and business networking across communities
- Reduced access to mainstream economic institutions

ℬ

The Way Forward

Addressing these economic challenges requires a multi-faceted approach involving policy reforms, improved access to financial services, and efforts to combat discrimination in housing and employment. The role of civil society organizations and business associations in bridging these gaps has become increasingly important.

Success in countering economic marginalization will require:

- Enhanced financial inclusion initiatives
- Anti-discrimination measures in housing and employment
- Support for entrepreneurship and skill development
- Improved access to quality education and professional training

The economic integration and prosperity of all communities, including minorities, is crucial for India's overall economic growth and social harmony. Addressing these challenges requires sustained effort from both policy makers and civil society to ensure equitable economic opportunities for all citizens.

XV

Building Bridges Across Indian Faiths

India's journey toward complete national integration faces complex challenges rooted in historical events, religious differences, and social structures. The relationship between Hindus, Muslims, and Christians requires careful navigation to build a more cohesive society while acknowledging past wounds and present realities.

The Muslim Community and Historical Memory

The Muslim community's integration into mainstream Indian society remains complicated by historical memories on both sides. While Hindus carry collective memories of invasion and religious persecution during certain periods of Muslim rule, some Muslims struggle with a diminished political influence following partition and the creation of

Pakistan. This mutual distrust needs to be addressed openly for genuine reconciliation to occur.

The Role of Religious Connections

The Khilafat Movement of the early 20th century exemplified how external religious affiliations could affect national unity. While religious connections to sacred sites like Mecca are integral to Islamic faith, the government's approach to religious subsidies deserves reassessment. Rather than supporting pilgrimages to foreign lands, promoting indigenous Islamic traditions like Sufism could strengthen Indian Muslims' connection to their homeland while preserving their religious identity.

Sufism as a Bridge

Sufism's syncretic traditions offer a promising path forward. The widespread acceptance of Sufi shrines in Indian villages, where Hindus and Muslims jointly celebrate festivals of Peers (saints), demonstrates the potential for interfaith harmony. This grassroots-level integration, where communities share in each other's joy and traditions, provides a model for broader social cohesion.

Contemporary Developments

The recent construction of the Ram Mandir in Ayodhya marks a significant moment in Hindu-Muslim relations. The relatively peaceful resolution of this long-standing dispute, despite its emotional charge, suggests that other contentious issues regarding religious sites could be resolved through dialogue and mutual understanding. Organizations like the RSS, which hold significant influence among Hindu communities, can play a crucial role in this process. When leaders like Mohan Bhagwat advocate for restraint and respect toward Muslim places of worship, it sends a powerful message to their followers.

Christianity and Social Justice

The challenge of Christian integration presents different dynamics. Christianity in India often intersects with caste issues, as many converts come from historically oppressed communities seeking escape from social discrimination. This highlights how religious conversion in India isn't merely a matter of faith but often a response to social inequality. Addressing caste discrimination becomes crucial not only for social justice but also for maintaining religious harmony.

Steps Toward Integration

For meaningful integration, several concrete steps deserve consideration:

1. Educational institutions should promote understanding of diverse religious traditions within India. This includes teaching about Sufism, indigenous Christian communities, and regional Hindu traditions that demonstrate religious syncretism. Understanding how different faiths have coexisted and influenced each other throughout Indian history can help counter divisive narratives.

2. Local governments should actively support interfaith celebrations and cultural exchanges. When communities celebrate festivals together, share meals, and participate in each other's traditions, it creates personal bonds that transcend religious differences. These interactions help dispel stereotypes and build lasting relationships.

3. Religious organizations need to take proactive steps toward dialogue and cooperation. Hindu organizations could reach out to Muslim and Christian communities not just for dialogue but for collaborative social work. Joint community service projects can build trust while benefiting society as a whole.

4. Media and public discourse should highlight positive examples of interfaith harmony rather than focusing exclusively on conflicts. Stories of communities helping each other during crises, celebrating together, and resolving differences peacefully can provide models for others to emulate.

The issue of religious conversions requires particular sensitivity. While freedom of religion is a constitutional right, addressing the social conditions that drive conversions is equally important. This means confronting caste discrimination directly through both legal enforcement and social reform. Religious leaders from all communities should work together to promote social equality and justice.

૪૭

The Path Forward

Economic integration is crucial. Ensuring equal access to education, employment, and business opportunities across religious communities can help reduce social tensions. When communities prosper together, they're more likely to maintain harmonious relationships.

India's strength lies in its diversity, and its future depends on successfully integrating all religious communities while respecting their unique identities. This requires moving beyond mere tolerance to active appreciation of different faiths and cultures. Rather than seeking uniformity, the goal should be unity in diversity – where each community maintains its distinctive character while identifying strongly as Indian.

The path forward requires patience, persistence, and goodwill from all communities. Religious leaders, civil society organizations, and government institutions must work together to build bridges of understanding. While historical wounds cannot be forgotten, they shouldn't prevent the creation of a more integrated and harmonious future. By promoting indigenous traditions of religious harmony, addressing social inequalities, and encouraging interfaith dialogue and cooperation, India can strengthen its national fabric while preserving its rich religious diversity.

XVI

The Rise of the Middle Class and the Fall of Collective Consciousness

The rise of the IT sector and the expansion of economic opportunities in post-liberalization India have profoundly reshaped the nation's social fabric, creating a complex interplay between stability, progress, and the erosion of collective social engagement. While the IT revolution has been a catalyst for economic growth and social mobility, it has also introduced new challenges, particularly in the realm of social and political activism. This transformation has not only dampened the potential for mass movements but also redefined the calculus of social engagement, leaving India at a crossroads between individual aspiration and collective responsibility.

☙

The Historical Context of Social Unrest

In the 1970s and 1980s, India was marked by limited economic opportunities and deep-seated social inequalities. Movements like Naxalism emerged as radical responses to systemic injustices, offering an outlet for those marginalized by the prevailing social and economic structures. At the time, the opportunity cost of political activism was negligible. For many, joining revolutionary movements was not just a choice but a necessity, as they had little to lose and everything to gain by challenging the status quo.

Grievances such as landlord exploitation, caste-based oppression, and economic disenfranchisement fueled these movements. With few avenues for upward mobility, activism became a viable path for those seeking justice and change. The absence of economic alternatives meant that radical engagement carried minimal personal risk, making it an attractive option for the disenfranchised.

☙

The Transformative Power of Economic Opportunities

The advent of the IT sector in the 1990s and 2000s fundamentally altered this dynamic. For the first time, millions of young Indians, regardless of caste, region, or socioeconomic background, gained access to unprecedented opportunities for social and economic advancement. The IT boom not only created jobs but also fostered a culture of aspiration and competition, transforming the social landscape.

This shift was driven by a powerful mechanism: community-driven aspiration. When one individual from a village or small town secured a job in the IT sector, it inspired others to follow suit. Education, skill development, and professional success became the new benchmarks of social mobility. The IT sector, with its promise of lucrative careers and global exposure, redefined the aspirations of an entire generation, shifting the focus from collective struggle to individual achievement.

ℬ

The New Calculus of Social Engagement

The economic opportunities created by the IT revolution have introduced a new calculus for social and political engagement. Participation in radical movements now comes with significant economic costs. For many, the risks of activism—such as losing lucrative career opportunities, jeopardizing chances for international emigration, or facing legal repercussions—far outweigh the potential benefits.

This shift has created a powerful deterrent to sustained social activism. The middle class, in particular, has become increasingly risk-averse, prioritizing personal financial stability and professional growth over collective action. The result is a society where economic considerations often trump social and political engagement, leaving little room for the kind of sustained movements that characterized earlier decades.

ℬ

The Transformation of Social Movements

The changing dynamics of social engagement are evident in movements like Anna Hazare's anti-corruption campaign in the early 2010s. While these movements generated widespread enthusiasm, particularly among the middle class and youth, they were constrained by economic realities. Weekend activism became the norm, with participants unable or unwilling to commit to prolonged efforts for social change.

This paradox—high on sentiment but low on sustained commitment—highlights the challenges of mobilizing a society increasingly focused on individual economic trajectories. The middle class, while vocal in its support for reform, often lacks the willingness to make the sacrifices necessary for meaningful structural change.

The Paradox of Stability

The economic transformation driven by the IT sector has undeniably brought remarkable social stability. By providing alternative pathways for addressing grievances, it has channeled potentially disruptive energies into economic pursuits. Movements like Naxalism, once a significant threat, have been relegated to isolated pockets in tribal regions where economic opportunities remain scarce.

However, this stability has come at a cost. The erosion of collective social and political engagement has made it increasingly difficult to address systemic issues such as corruption, inequality, and environmental degradation. The very mechanisms that have pacified the broader social landscape have also weakened the traditional bases of social and political movements.

Challenges of Social Reform

One of the most significant casualties of this transformation has been the decline of activism in universities, once the crucibles of social and political change. Today, campuses are more focused on producing graduates equipped for the job market than on fostering a culture of dissent and reform. The "foot soldiers" of social change—individuals willing to dedicate time and resources to broader societal concerns—have become increasingly rare.

This shift has made political reform more challenging. As potential agents of change become more invested in their personal economic trajectories, the impetus for collective action has diminished. The result is a society that, while economically prosperous, struggles to address fundamental social and political challenges.

ॐ

Alternative Paths of Engagement

In this new landscape, reformists must explore innovative strategies to bring about social change. Digital activism, strategic media engagement, targeted legal interventions, and leveraging global networks have emerged as alternative mechanisms for exerting pressure on power structures. These tools offer new ways to mobilize support and advocate for reform, even in a society increasingly focused on individual economic success.

ॐ

Conclusion: A Delicate Balance

India finds itself in a precarious equilibrium. Economic stability has been achieved, but at the cost of collective social consciousness. The IT sector has fundamentally recalibrated social imagination, replacing collective struggle with individual aspiration.

The greatest irony lies in the unprecedented prosperity that has simultaneously created a society less capable of addressing fundamental social and political challenges. Social stability is desirable, but not at the expense of meaningful structural reform.

The future of Indian democracy depends on finding mechanisms to reignite collective social consciousness without compromising the economic gains of the past decades – reconciling individual economic aspirations with broader social responsibilities.

XVII

Anti-Caste Movements: Evolving Sympathies and Challenges

In recent years, India's anti-caste movements have undergone a significant transformation. What began as a struggle for social justice and equality within the framework of Indian democracy has increasingly taken on a more radical tone, with many leaders and intellectuals openly critiquing Hinduism, aligning with leftist ideologies, and expressing sympathy for separatist movements in Kashmir and Naxal-affected regions. Figures like Kancha Ilaiah, Chandra Shekhar Azad, Jignesh Mevani, Umar Khalid, Gauri Lankesh, Arundhati Roy, and Kuffir have emerged as prominent voices in this evolving discourse. While their critiques of caste-based oppression remain central, their opposition to Hinduism, Hindutva, and the Indian state has sparked intense debate and controversy, often earning them the label of "anti-national" from the right wing.

ॐ

The Roots of Anti-Caste Movements

The anti-caste movement in India has its roots in the teachings of social reformers like Jyotirao Phule, Periyar E.V. Ramasamy, and Dr. B.R. Ambedkar. These leaders sought to dismantle the caste system, which they saw as a hierarchical and oppressive structure embedded in Hinduism. Their vision was one of social justice, equality, and empowerment for Dalits, Adivasis, and Other Backward Classes (OBCs).

In recent decades, this movement has gained momentum, with leaders like Kancha Ilaiah and Chandra Shekhar Azad taking up the mantle. Ilaiah, a Dalit-Bahujan intellectual, has been a vocal critic of Brahminical Hinduism, arguing that it is inherently oppressive and exclusionary. His works, such as Why I Am Not a Hindu, have become foundational texts for many anti-caste activists. Similarly, Azad, the founder of the Bhim Army, has mobilized Dalit youth to fight against caste-based discrimination and violence, often clashing with upper-caste dominance and Hindutva forces.

ॐ

From Anti-Caste to Anti-Hindu

As the anti-caste movement has grown, so too has its critique of Hinduism. Many activists argue that the religion's scriptures, rituals, and social structures are inherently biased in favor of upper castes, particularly Brahmins. This has led to a broader rejection of Hinduism and, by extension, Hindutva—the ideology that seeks to define Indian culture and identity in terms of Hindu values.

Kancha Ilaiah, for instance, has called for a "post-Hindu India," where Dalits and OBCs can free themselves from the shackles of Brahminical oppression. Similarly, Kuffir, a Dalit writer and blogger, has used his platform to critique Hinduism and promote anti-caste discourse. These voices argue that true liberation for marginalized communities can only be achieved by rejecting Hinduism altogether.

This shift has placed the anti-caste movement in direct opposition to the religious right, which views Hinduism as an integral part of Indian identity. The right wing accuses anti-caste activists of being "anti-Hindu" and, by extension, "anti-national," further polarizing the discourse.

Alignment with Leftist Ideologies

In their opposition to the right wing, many anti-caste activists have found common cause with leftist ideologies. They argue that socialism and communism offer a more equitable framework for addressing caste-based and class-based inequalities. This alignment has led to collaborations with leftist parties and movements, as well as a critique of neoliberal economic policies that they believe disproportionately benefit upper castes and corporate elites.

Jignesh Mevani, a Dalit leader and MLA from Gujarat, is a prominent example of this trend. Mevani rose to prominence during the 2016 Una Dalit uprising and has consistently criticized the BJP and Hindutva forces for their alleged complicity in caste-based violence. He aligns himself with leftist politics and has called for unity among Dalits, OBCs, and minorities to challenge the ruling establishment.

Similarly, Umar Khalid, a former student leader from Jawaharlal Nehru University (JNU), has expressed solidarity with Dalit and Adivasi movements while critiquing Hindutva and communalism. Khalid's participation in protests against the Citizenship Amendment Act (CAA) and the National Register of Citizens (NRC) has made him a target of the right wing, which labels him as "anti-national."

Sympathy for Separatist Movements

One of the most controversial aspects of the anti-caste movement's transformation has been its sympathy for separatist movements, particularly in Kashmir and Naxal-affected regions. Many activists argue that the struggles of Kashmiris and Naxalites mirror their own fight against oppression. They see these movements as part of a broader struggle for self-determination and justice against a repressive state.

Arundhati Roy, a prominent writer and activist, has been a vocal supporter of Kashmiri self-determination and has criticized the Indian government's policies in the region. Roy's essays and speeches often highlight the parallels between the oppression faced by Dalits, Adivasis, and Kashmiris, framing them as part of a larger struggle against state violence and injustice.

Similarly, the late Gauri Lankesh, a journalist and activist, was a fierce critic of Hindutva and caste-based discrimination. Through her Kannada weekly, Gauri Lankesh Patrike, she exposed the injustices faced by Dalits,

Adivasis, and other marginalized communities. Lankesh also expressed sympathy for Naxalites, viewing their armed struggle as a response to state repression and economic exploitation.

౮

The "Anti-National" Label

The right wing's use of the term "anti-national" to describe anti-caste activists and their allies reflects the deep ideological divide in contemporary Indian politics. For the right wing, nationalism is closely tied to Hinduism and Hindutva, and any critique of these is seen as an attack on the nation itself. Anti-caste activists, on the other hand, argue that true nationalism must include social justice and equality for all, regardless of caste, creed, or religion.

This labeling has significant implications for the discourse around caste and nationalism in India. It marginalizes anti-caste voices and delegitimizes their struggles, framing them as enemies of the state rather than as citizens fighting for their rights. At the same time, it reinforces the right wing's narrative of a unified Hindu nation under threat from internal and external forces.

౮

Conclusion

The transformation of anti-caste movements into broader critiques of Hinduism, Hindutva, and the Indian state represents a profound challenge to India's social and political order. While these movements have brought much-needed attention to the enduring inequalities of the caste system, their alignment with leftist ideologies and separatist movements has sparked intense ideological and political conflicts.

As India continues to grapple with these tensions, the struggle for social justice and equality remains as urgent as ever. The question is whether the nation can find a way to address these deep-seated issues without further fracturing its social and political fabric. The anti-caste movement's evolution underscores the complexity of this challenge, highlighting the need for a more inclusive and equitable vision of Indian democracy.

XVIII

The North-South Divide: Political Implications of Demographic and Economic Disparities

India has long grappled with regional disparities. Among the most pronounced divides is that between the northern and southern states, which differ significantly in terms of demographics, economic contributions, and political representation. These disparities are not just statistical curiosities; they have profound implications for India's federal structure, governance, and national unity. As the southern states face a declining population growth rate and the northern states continue to grow, the resulting political and economic tensions threaten to exacerbate regional strife.

ॐ

Demographic Divergence: A Looming Political Crisis

One of the most striking differences between India's northern and southern states is their demographic trajectories. Southern states such as Tamil Nadu, Kerala, Karnataka, and Andhra Pradesh have achieved population growth rates below the replacement level, a sign of successful family planning, higher literacy rates, and better healthcare. In contrast, northern states like Uttar Pradesh, Bihar, Rajasthan, and Madhya Pradesh continue to experience high population growth, driven by higher fertility rates and slower progress in social development.

This demographic divergence has significant political implications, particularly in the context of parliamentary constituency delimitation. The Indian Constitution mandates that the number of Lok Sabha seats allocated to each state be revised periodically based on population data. The last delimitation exercise was conducted in 1976, and the next one, postponed until 2026, is expected to reallocate seats based on the latest population figures.

If the delimitation proceeds as planned, southern states, with their declining population shares, are likely to lose parliamentary seats, while northern states, with their growing populations, will gain representation. This shift could drastically alter the balance of power in the Lok Sabha, reducing the political influence of the more developed southern states. Critics argue that this would punish states that have successfully managed their population growth and invested in human development, while rewarding those that have lagged behind.

ॐ

Economic Contributions vs. Fiscal Returns: A Growing Resentment

The southern states are not just demographic outliers; they are also economic powerhouses. States like Tamil Nadu, Karnataka, and Telangana contribute disproportionately to India's GDP, driven by their robust industrial bases, thriving IT sectors, and higher levels of urbanization. For instance, Karnataka, home to India's Silicon Valley, Bangalore, is a global hub for technology and innovation. Similarly, Tamil Nadu is a manufacturing powerhouse, contributing significantly to India's exports.

However, the fiscal returns these states receive from the central government are not commensurate with their economic contributions. India's federal tax redistribution mechanism, governed by the Finance Commission, allocates funds to states based on a formula that considers factors like population, income levels, and development indicators. As a result, poorer states, often referred to as the BIMARU states (Bihar, Madhya Pradesh, Rajasthan, and Uttar Pradesh), receive a larger share of central funds due to their lower per capita income and higher levels of backwardness.

While this redistribution is intended to promote equity and reduce regional disparities, it has led to growing resentment in the south. Southern states argue that they are being penalized for their economic success and efficient governance, while states that have failed to curb population growth or improve development indicators are rewarded with greater financial support. This perception of "good behavior being punished and bad behavior being rewarded" has fueled calls for a more equitable and performance-based allocation of resources.

ॐ

Political Implications: Regional Strife and Federal Tensions

The combination of demographic shifts and fiscal imbalances has the potential to ignite regional strife and strain India's federal structure. Southern states, already feeling marginalized, may intensify their demands for greater autonomy and a fairer share of resources. Movements advocating for federalism and state rights, such as the calls for "Dravidian pride" in Tamil Nadu, could gain momentum, further polarizing the political landscape.

Moreover, the loss of political representation in the Lok Sabha could diminish the south's ability to influence national policies, particularly those related to economic reforms, taxation, and resource allocation. This could lead to a sense of alienation and disenchantment among the southern populace, undermining the spirit of cooperative federalism that is essential for India's unity and progress.

ॐ

The Way Forward: Balancing Equity and Incentives

To address these challenges, India must adopt a nuanced approach that balances equity with incentives for good governance. The criteria for resource allocation should be revised to reward states that achieve social and economic milestones, such as population stabilization, improved literacy rates, and better healthcare outcomes. Additionally, the delimitation process could consider factors beyond population, such as economic contributions and development indicators, to ensure a fairer distribution of political power.

Dialogue and consensus-building will be critical in navigating these complex issues. The central government must engage with state governments, particularly those in the south, to address their concerns and foster a sense of inclusion. By promoting cooperative federalism and recognizing the diverse contributions of all regions, India can mitigate the risks of regional strife and build a more cohesive and equitable nation.

Conclusion

The disparities between India's northern and southern states are not merely regional differences; they are a reflection of deeper demographic, economic, and political dynamics. As the south grapples with declining population growth and diminishing political clout, and the north continues to grow in numbers and influence, the need for a balanced and inclusive approach has never been more urgent. By addressing these disparities with fairness and foresight, India can ensure that its federal structure remains robust and its unity intact, even in the face of growing regional challenges.

XIX

Politicians, Government Employees, and the Alienation of the Ordinary Citizen

Beneath the vibrant façade of India's democracy and cultural diversity lies a troubling reality—a profound imbalance of power that defines the daily lives of its citizens. Power and influence are disproportionately concentrated in the hands of government employees and politicians, while the ordinary citizen remains disempowered and vulnerable.

The Concentration of Power

Government employees, from high-ranking bureaucrats to lower-level officials, control the implementation of policies, allocation of resources, and delivery of public services. Their decisions can determine the fate of individuals, businesses, and communities. Similarly, politicians influence policy-making, allocate funds, and often act as gatekeepers to opportunities and resources.

This concentration of power creates a system where the ordinary citizen must navigate a labyrinth of bureaucratic procedures to access basic services such as healthcare, education, or legal redress. The discretion exercised by government officials can mean the difference between timely assistance and endless delays. This dynamic places the ordinary citizen in a position of vulnerability, dependent on the goodwill and efficiency of these two powerful classes.

ಐ

The Government as an Enabler of the Powerful

A common perception among Indians is that the government functions primarily for the benefit of its employees and politicians rather than ordinary citizens. Government employees enjoy job security, pensions, and benefits often unmatched in the private sector. Politicians wield significant influence and frequently amass wealth and power during their tenure. The system appears designed to protect and empower these groups, while the needs of ordinary citizens are frequently sidelined.

Government employees are rarely held accountable for inefficiency or corruption, and politicians often escape scrutiny for misuse of power. The lack of transparency and accountability in governance further exacerbates this imbalance. The ordinary citizen, lacking resources or influence, must navigate a system that seems indifferent to their plight, leading to widespread disillusionment and a sense of disenfranchisement.

℥

The Vulnerability of the Ordinary Citizen

This power disparity has profound implications for Indian society. Ordinary citizens often find themselves at the mercy of these two classes, with limited recourse when faced with injustice or neglect. A farmer seeking compensation for crop loss, a student applying for a scholarship, or a small business owner seeking a license must rely on the discretion of government officials and the influence of local politicians.

Moreover, this concentration of power undermines democracy's foundational principle of equal representation and participation. Despite being the backbone of the nation, ordinary citizens often feel excluded from the decision-making processes that shape their lives.

℥

The Clamor for Government Jobs and Political Power

Given this power imbalance, it is unsurprising that there is intense competition for government positions and political influence. Government jobs offer stability, benefits, and a level of discretion unmatched in the private sector. For many, such positions represent not just livelihood but a way to gain a foothold in the system and escape the vulnerability of being an ordinary citizen.

Similarly, political power is highly sought after as it offers control over resources and influence over decision-making. Politicians are often seen as ultimate arbiters of power, capable of shaping the lives of millions. The allure of political power is reinforced by the wealth and status that frequently accompany it.

‍ℰ

The Alienation of Certain Classes

While government jobs and political power are universally desirable, access to these positions is not equally distributed. For middle-class youth, particularly those from upper castes, the competition for government jobs is fierce. The system of caste-based reservation quotas, while aimed at addressing historical injustices, has further limited opportunities for those outside reserved categories.

The barriers to entering politics are even higher, often requiring significant financial resources and political connections. For those without these advantages, the dream of political power remains elusive. This exclusion leads to a sense of alienation among certain classes who feel the system is stacked against them despite their qualifications and aspirations.

‍ℰ

The Escape to Foreign Shores

Faced with limited opportunities for empowerment within India, many talented young people choose to seek their fortunes abroad. Countries like the United States, Canada, and European nations offer not only better economic prospects but also a sense of dignity and respect. In these nations, individuals are judged more on merit and treated as equals, without needing to appease government employees or politicians.

This brain drain represents a significant loss for India as some of its most talented and ambitious youth build their lives elsewhere. While they may achieve financial success and personal fulfillment abroad, their absence leaves a void in India's social and economic fabric, depriving the country of their potential contributions to progress and reform.

Conclusion: A Call for Systemic Change

The concentration of power in the hands of government employees and politicians, and the resulting disempowerment of ordinary citizens, demands attention. Creating a more equitable system requires systemic changes, including bureaucratic reforms, greater governance transparency, and efforts to level the political playing field.

It also calls for a shift in societal attitudes away from the glorification of power and status toward a culture that values merit, dignity, and equal opportunity. Only by addressing these issues can India hope to stem the tide of alienation and brain drain, creating a society where every citizen feels empowered to contribute to the nation's progress. While challenging, this transformation is essential if India is to fulfill its promise as a truly inclusive and democratic nation.

Political Dynamics and Opposition Challenges

This section focuses on India's political landscape, including the BJP's dominance, the struggles of the opposition, and the challenges of maintaining political pluralism.

XX

Political Persecution or Strategic Containment? The AAP-BJP Confrontation

The recent spate of legal actions against Aam Aadmi Party (AAP) leaders, culminating in the arrest of Delhi Chief Minister Arvind Kejriwal, has thrust into sharp focus the intricate political dynamics between India's ruling Bharatiya Janata Party (BJP) and the rising political alternative represented by AAP.

What appears on the surface as a series of judicial proceedings reveals a deeper strategic calculus by the BJP to systematically disrupt AAP's growing political momentum. The party's leadership seems acutely aware that AAP represents a more nuanced and potentially more dangerous political challenge than the traditional opposition, the Indian National Congress.

ೞ

The Rapid Rise of AAP

AAP's political trajectory has been remarkable. From its origins as an anti-corruption movement to establishing governments in key states like Delhi and Punjab, the party has demonstrated a capacity for rapid growth and political innovation. Its success in urban centers and ability to connect with younger, more aspirational voters has been particularly noteworthy.

The party's governance model, characterized by focused interventions in education, healthcare, and public infrastructure, has resonated with urban middle-class voters. In Delhi, Kejriwal's government's initiatives in school education and healthcare have been widely appreciated, creating a template that could be replicated in other states.

ೞ

Strategic Threat Perception

The BJP's aggressive legal actions against AAP leaders can be interpreted as a preemptive strategic move. By targeting key leadership through various investigative agencies, the party aims to destabilize AAP before it can consolidate its national footprint.

The political arithmetic is clear. AAP has already established a strong presence in Delhi and Punjab and shows promising signs of expansion in states like Haryana,

Gujarat, and Goa. Its potential to emerge as a third significant national force—beyond the BJP and Congress—is what seems to be causing significant concern in BJP's strategic circles.

Unlike the Congress, which is perceived as a declining force, AAP represents a more dynamic and adaptable political alternative. Its leadership is younger, its approach more technocratic, and its appeal crosses traditional caste and regional boundaries.

ಜ

Political Positioning and Hindu Voter Outreach

What distinguishes Arvind Kejriwal from other opposition leaders, particularly Rahul Gandhi, is his nuanced approach to Hindu voter sentiment. While Gandhi has often been perceived as either indifferent or antagonistic to Hindu cultural sensibilities, Kejriwal has demonstrated a more politically astute understanding of India's religious landscape.

Kejriwal has strategically positioned himself as a leader who respects Hindu traditions while maintaining a secular political framework. Unlike the Congress party's approach, which often seemed defensive or dismissive of Hindu cultural concerns, AAP under Kejriwal has skillfully made overtures that resonate with the Hindu majority.

The BJP recognizes this subtle but significant shift. Kejriwal's ability to speak the language of Hindu cultural pride while maintaining a progressive governance model represents a more sophisticated political challenge.

ಜ

Legal Actions: A Political Tool

The series of investigations and arrests targeting AAP leaders suggest a coordinated approach to politically neutralize the party. While legal processes must be respected, the timing and intensity of these actions raise legitimate questions about their motivations.

The arrest of Arvind Kejriwal in the Delhi excise policy case, which came after multiple other AAP leaders were sent to jail, appears more politically motivated than purely legal. The selective nature of these investigations, when many leaders from other parties facing serious corruption allegations remain unscathed, further reinforces this perception.

☙

Broader Political Implications

The BJP's strategy reveals a long-term view of India's political landscape. By 2034, the party seems to calculate that AAP could potentially emerge as a significant challenger, particularly in urban and semi-urban constituencies where traditional political alignments are rapidly transforming.

The method appears to be one of political containment—using legal and investigative mechanisms to prevent AAP from building momentum and expanding its organizational infrastructure. By keeping key leaders engaged in legal battles, the party hopes to dissipate AAP's political energy and resources.

☙

AAP's Potential Response

For AAP, these challenges present both a threat and an opportunity. The party can potentially position these legal actions as political vendetta, appealing to voters' sense of fairness and democratic principles. However, it will require sophisticated political messaging and continued focus on governance and grassroots connection.

The party's leadership will need to balance legal challenges with continued political mobilization, ensuring that these legal battles do not completely derail their organizational expansion and political narrative.

Conclusion

The current confrontation between BJP and AAP is more than just a legal dispute. It represents a significant moment in India's evolving political landscape, where new political formations are challenging established power structures.

The outcomes of these legal proceedings and political maneuvers will have profound implications for India's democratic discourse and the potential emergence of alternative political narratives.

While the immediate battlefield appears to be in courtrooms and investigation agencies, the real contest is for the political imagination of India's emerging voter demographic—young, aspirational, and increasingly impatient with traditional political frameworks.

XXI

Rahul Gandhi and Congress's Path to Reconnect with India's Majority

The Congress party faces an existential challenge in modern Indian politics. Once the dominant force that shaped India's post-independence trajectory, it now struggles with fundamental issues of national identity, security, and cultural aspirations. The path to political revival requires addressing several critical challenges that have eroded its connection with the Indian electorate.

The Hindu Voter Crisis

The party has significantly alienated its Hindu voter base through its positions on key issues. Its ambivalent stance on the abrogation of Article 370 in Kashmir and perceived lack of support for the Ram Temple in Ayodhya have damaged its credibility with this crucial demographic. Rahul Gandhi's statements about Hindu extremism have further widened this gap, creating a perception that the party is disconnected from Hindu cultural aspirations and religious sentiments.

∞

National Security Weakness

On national security, Congress appears weak and indecisive, particularly regarding China. The electorate demands clear, strong positions on territorial integrity and defense, but the party's diplomatic approach is seen as too soft when confronted with direct challenges to India's sovereignty. This perception must change for Congress to be taken seriously as a national alternative.

∞

The Corruption Legacy

The corruption scandals of previous Congress governments continue to haunt the party. While the BJP faces its own corruption allegations, Congress has failed to present a convincing case that it would govern differently. The party needs to acknowledge past failures and present specific, credible plans for clean governance that go beyond mere criticism of the current administration.

∞

The Minority Question

Congress's approach to minority issues has backfired significantly. While protecting minority rights remains important, the party's policies are widely seen as appeasement rather than genuine secularism. This has cost them Hindu votes without necessarily securing minority support. The party needs a new framework that protects minorities while respecting majority sentiments.

Development and Progress

The party's stance on development projects appears muddled and often anti-progress. When foreign-funded NGOs protest against mining, nuclear power, or infrastructure projects, Congress's ambiguous position hurts India's development interests. The party must articulate clear policies that balance progress with environmental concerns.

Leadership Crisis

Rahul Gandhi's leadership style requires a complete overhaul. His statements often appear disconnected from ground realities and voter concerns. The Congress leader needs to demonstrate understanding and respect for Hindu cultural aspirations while maintaining secular principles. His communication must shift from criticism to constructive alternatives that resonate with the electorate.

Economic Vision

On the economic front, criticizing Modi's policies isn't enough. Congress must present a detailed alternative vision that addresses both growth and equity. This includes clear policies on job creation, industrial development, agricultural reform, foreign investment, and infrastructure development. The party needs to convince voters it can deliver better economic outcomes while maintaining social harmony.

৪০

The Bottom Line

To chart a viable path forward, Congress must undertake several fundamental changes. It needs to take a clear stand supporting Kashmir's integration and acknowledge the legitimacy of Hindu cultural symbols. The party must present a strong national security doctrine, particularly regarding China, and develop specific anti-corruption measures that rebuild public trust. Most importantly, it must redefine secularism to include respect for majority religious sentiments while protecting minority rights.

Until Congress makes these substantive changes, BJP will likely maintain its dominance regardless of its shortcomings. The party's revival depends not on attacking Modi but on rebuilding trust with voters who have rejected its current approach. The real test for Rahul Gandhi and Congress isn't just criticizing the current government - it's proving they can offer better governance while respecting India's cultural and security interests. Without this fundamental transformation, talks of returning to power will remain wishful thinking.

The path forward requires not a wholesale abandonment of core principles but their thoughtful reformation and contemporary expression. Congress must convince voters it can protect both India's secular fabric and its cultural heritage, promote both economic growth and social justice, and ensure both national security and diplomatic engagement. The choice is clear: change significantly or remain politically marginalized.

XXII

Wrong Battles, Missed Opportunities: India's Opposition and Economic Reform

The current opposition, led by Rahul Gandhi and the Congress party, appears to be missing opportunities to challenge the Modi government on substantial economic policy matters while advocating for potentially regressive measures that could harm India's economic prospects.

Growth Challenges and Missed Opportunities

The Modi government's economic performance presents several legitimate areas for critique. While India maintains respectable GDP growth of 5-6%, this falls short of the 8-10% growth rate many economists consider necessary for India to achieve middle-income status and effectively compete with China. The promised agenda of "minimum government, maximum governance" has seen limited implementation, with reform momentum slowing compared to the liberalization era initiated by PV Narasimha Rao and advanced under Atal Bihari Vajpayee.

ॐ

Agricultural Reform and Economic Modernization

Yet rather than focusing on these substantive issues, the opposition's economic narrative has often taken counterproductive directions. A prime example is their stance on agricultural reforms. When the Modi government introduced farm laws aimed at modernizing India's agricultural sector by allowing greater market participation and reducing intermediary bottlenecks, the opposition chose to oppose these reforms wholesale rather than engaging in constructive criticism to improve them. While the implementation approach of these reforms deserved scrutiny, the opposition's blanket rejection ignored the fundamental need for agricultural modernization.

ॐ

The Pension System Dilemma

Perhaps more concerning is the opposition's advocacy for reverting to the Old Pension Scheme (OPS) from the National Pension System (NPS) introduced during the Vajpayee era. The NPS was implemented precisely to address the unsustainable fiscal burden of the OPS on state finances. Several opposition-ruled states have already announced returns to OPS, despite warnings from economists about its severe long-term implications for fiscal health.

₧

Labor Reform and Privatization Challenges

The opposition's approach to labor reforms has been similarly problematic. While the Modi government's pace of labor reform has been criticized as insufficient, the opposition has often aligned with unions resisting any significant changes to India's complex labor laws. This stance ignores the need to create a more flexible labor market that could boost formal sector employment and manufacturing competitiveness.

On privatization, while the opposition rightly points out the slow pace of PSU disinvestment under Modi (with Air India being a notable exception), their own policy statements suggest an even more conservative approach to public sector reform. This represents a missed opportunity to push for more efficient management of public assets while ensuring fair labor transitions.

The opposition could instead focus on several critical areas where the government's performance warrants serious scrutiny:

1. **Approach to regulatory reform** - Despite promises of ease of doing business, India's regulatory environment remains complex, with multiple layers of compliance requirements that burden businesses, particularly SMEs. The opposition could advocate for specific regulatory streamlining while ensuring adequate

protections remain in place.

2. **Inadequate progress in education and healthcare reform** - These sectors are crucial for improving human capital and productivity, yet comprehensive reform proposals have been lacking. The opposition could present alternative policies focusing on improving educational outcomes and healthcare access while maintaining fiscal responsibility.

3. **Pace and direction of financial sector reforms** - The Modi government's approach to banking reform has largely focused on consolidation rather than fundamental restructuring – merging weaker public sector banks with stronger ones and transferring PSU assets between public entities. While this may create larger banks, it doesn't address the core issues of efficiency, governance, and political interference in lending decisions. The opposition could push for genuine privatization of public sector banks, which currently control about two-thirds of India's banking assets. The government's reluctance to reduce its banking sector presence perpetuates a system that often leads to inefficient capital allocation and periodic recapitalization burdens on taxpayers.

4. **Urban development policies** - Despite the Smart Cities Mission, India's urban infrastructure remains inadequate for its growing population. The opposition could advocate for comprehensive urban reform, including better land use regulations and affordable housing solutions to address the urbanization challenges.

5. **International trade stance** - While "Make in India" aims to boost manufacturing, India's cautious approach to international trade agreements, exemplified by its RCEP

withdrawal, may be limiting economic opportunities. The opposition could push for more strategic trade integration while ensuring adequate domestic safeguards.

Instead, much of the opposition's economic discourse has centered on criticism of specific initiatives like demonetization or GST implementation, without presenting coherent alternative policies.

The opposition's approach appears to reflect a broader challenge in Indian politics: the tendency to prioritize short-term political gains over long-term economic vision. This is particularly evident in their support for subsidies and welfare schemes without adequate attention to fiscal sustainability or economic efficiency.

ॐ

The Way Forward

For India to achieve its economic potential, it needs an opposition that can effectively challenge the government on substantive policy issues while presenting credible alternative approaches. The current situation, where the opposition often advocates for economically regressive policies while missing opportunities for substantive criticism of the government's reform agenda, does little to advance India's economic discourse or progress.

XXIII

The Three Pillars of Electoral Success in India

In the complex landscape of Indian democracy, political success often hinges on a delicate balance of three fundamental pillars: muscle, money, and intellectual capability. This framework provides a fascinating lens through which to understand why some political parties thrive while others falter, despite seemingly noble intentions and strong ideological foundations.

Muscle Power

In India's semi-feudal democratic setup, muscle power remains a crucial element of political influence. This doesn't necessarily translate to outright violence or intimidation, but rather manifests as a demonstration of organizational strength and the ability to mobilize masses.

Political parties must project an image of authority and protection, particularly in regions where state institutions may be perceived as weak or ineffective.

When voters evaluate political parties, they often look for signs that the party can effectively represent and protect their interests. This perception of strength becomes particularly important in rural and semi-urban areas, where traditional power structures continue to hold sway. The ability to organize large rallies, maintain a strong cadre base, and demonstrate street presence all contribute to this aspect of political power.

ॐ

Money Power

Financial resources form the second pillar of political success in India. The scale of Indian elections, combined with the need for extensive campaigning across diverse geographical regions, demands substantial financial backing. Money power isn't just about funding election campaigns; it's about maintaining a year-round political machinery, supporting party workers, and building organizational infrastructure.

Modern political campaigns require sophisticated communication strategies, media presence, and technological tools - all of which demand significant financial investment. Moreover, welfare schemes and community development programs, often crucial for building voter base, require robust financial backing. Parties without adequate financial resources often struggle to maintain visibility and relevance between elections.

ॐ

Intellectual Power

The third essential component is intellectual power - the ability to articulate a compelling ideology, frame narratives, and develop policies that resonate with the electorate. This aspect involves not just having good ideas, but also the capability to communicate them effectively and translate them into actionable programs that appeal to various segments of society.

Intellectual power enables parties to:

- Develop coherent policy frameworks
- Create effective communication strategies
- Build convincing narratives around their vision
- Formulate solutions to complex socio-economic challenges
- Engage meaningfully with different stakeholder groups

ॐ

Case Studies in Success and Failure

- **The Success of TRS in Telangana**: The Telangana Rashtra Samithi (now BRS) exemplifies the successful integration of all three powers. The party demonstrated muscle power through its ability to mobilize massive protests during the Telangana movement. Its financial strength grew with support from influential business groups and strategic resource management. Intellectually, it successfully framed the Telangana statehood narrative and later transformed it into a governance agenda, showing remarkable adaptability in its political messaging.
- **Shiv Sena's Rise in Maharashtra**: Shiv Sena's trajectory in Maharashtra similarly illustrates this triple power

dynamic. The party built its foundation on strong street presence and organizational muscle, particularly in Mumbai. Its alliances with business interests ensured financial stability, while its intellectual framework - though often criticized - successfully merged regional pride with practical governance concerns, creating a distinct political identity.

The Lok Satta Party Experience

In contrast, the Lok Satta Party, despite its strong intellectual foundation and policy expertise, struggled to achieve electoral success in Andhra Pradesh and Telangana. While the party had excellent ideas for governance reforms and anti-corruption measures, it lacked both the muscle power to establish a strong ground presence and the financial resources to sustain long-term political activities. This case demonstrates how even the most well-conceived political platforms can fail without the support of other power components.

The Way Forward

This analysis raises important questions about the nature of Indian democracy and its future evolution. While the current reality demands this triple power approach, there's hope that as democratic institutions mature and voter awareness increases, the relative importance of muscle and money power might diminish in favor of intellectual and policy-based politics.

However, for the foreseeable future, political parties must recognize that success in Indian politics requires a balanced approach incorporating all three power elements. Those aspiring to create political change must work within this framework while simultaneously working to transform it. This might involve:

- Building strong but legal organizational networks
- Developing sustainable funding models
- Investing in policy research and communication
- Creating innovative ways to connect with voters
- Maintaining ethical standards while acknowledging political realities

The challenge for emerging political forces is to find this balance without compromising their core values or contributing to the perpetuation of problematic aspects of the current system. Success in Indian politics thus becomes not just about accumulating power, but about wielding it responsibly while working towards systemic improvement.

XXIV

BJP's Quest for Dominance: Stifling Regional Parties and Undermining Political Pluralism

Since Narendra Modi assumed power in 2014, the Bharatiya Janata Party (BJP) has embarked on an unprecedented political expansion, often likened to an "Ashwamedha yagna" in its relentless pursuit of dominance across India. This expansion, however, has come at a significant cost to the country's political pluralism, with regional parties bearing the brunt of the BJP's aggressive strategies. The party's tactics, which include leveraging central investigative agencies and exploiting leadership vacuums in rival parties, have reshaped India's political landscape, raising concerns about the erosion of democratic norms and the rise of a de facto single-party system.

※

The BJP's Playbook: Targeting Regional and Dynastic Parties

The BJP's rise to dominance has been marked by a calculated focus on weakening regional parties, particularly those that are dynastic or in the midst of leadership transitions. Parties like the Shiv Sena, which lost its charismatic founder Bal Thackeray, and the Telugu Desam Party (TDP), which faces challenges in leadership succession, have been prime targets. The BJP has exploited internal fissures within these parties, often engineering splits or poaching key leaders to destabilize them. The recent fragmentation of the Shiv Sena in Maharashtra and the BJP's subsequent alliance with a faction led by Eknath Shinde exemplify this strategy.

In states like Telangana and Tamil Nadu, where the BJP has historically been weak, the party is making concerted efforts to expand its footprint. While it has achieved significant success in Karnataka, its attempts to penetrate Telangana and Tamil Nadu have been met with mixed results. Nevertheless, the BJP's relentless campaigning, coupled with its ability to co-opt local leaders and narratives, suggests that it is only a matter of time before it makes deeper inroads into these regions.

※

The Role of Central Agencies in Political Persecution

A key instrument in the BJP's political arsenal has been the use of central investigative agencies such as the Enforcement Directorate (ED), the Central Bureau of Investigation (CBI), and the Income Tax Department. Opposition leaders and regional party figures have frequently found themselves under investigation, often coinciding with critical political moments. Critics argue that these agencies are being weaponized to intimidate and silence political opponents, thereby undermining the principles of fair play and justice.

For instance, leaders from the Trinamool Congress (TMC) in West Bengal, the Aam Aadmi Party (AAP) in Delhi, and the Nationalist Congress Party (NCP) in Maharashtra have faced raids and investigations, which many view as politically motivated. This systematic targeting of opposition figures has created an atmosphere of fear, discouraging dissent and consolidating the BJP's hold on power.

ॐ

The Weakening of Congress and the Rise of a Single-Party Dominance

The decline of the Indian National Congress, once the dominant force in Indian politics, has further accelerated the BJP's ascendancy. With the Congress struggling to reinvent itself and regain public trust, the opposition space has become fragmented and ineffective. This vacuum has allowed the BJP to consolidate its position, not just at the national level but also in states where regional parties once held sway.

The BJP's dominance is increasingly reminiscent of single-party systems seen in countries like China, where the Communist Party exercises unchallenged control. While

India remains a democracy in form, the concentration of power in the hands of one party raises concerns about the health of its democratic institutions. The erosion of federalism, the weakening of regional voices, and the marginalization of opposition parties threaten the pluralistic ethos that has long defined India's political identity.

৪৩

Anti-Constitutional Tactics and the Threat to Pluralism

The BJP's strategies, such as engineering splits in rival parties and using state machinery to target opponents, have often been criticized as anti-constitutional. These actions not only undermine the spirit of democracy but also weaken the checks and balances essential for a healthy political system. Regional parties, which have historically represented the diverse aspirations of India's states, are increasingly finding themselves marginalized, unable to withstand the BJP's onslaught.

This trend has significant implications for India's pluralism. Regional parties have played a crucial role in ensuring that the voices of India's diverse communities are heard in the corridors of power. Their decline risks homogenizing India's political discourse, reducing the space for regional aspirations and identities. In a country as diverse as India, this could have far-reaching consequences for social cohesion and national unity.

৪৩

The Road Ahead: A Decade of BJP Dominance?

The BJP's momentum shows no signs of slowing down. Having won three consecutive national elections, the party appears poised to dominate Indian politics for at least another decade, potentially until 2034. With a weakened opposition and a well-oiled political machinery, the BJP's grip on power seems unshakable for the foreseeable future.

However, this dominance comes at a cost. The erosion of pluralism, the weakening of democratic institutions, and the rise of a de facto single-party system threaten to alter the very fabric of Indian democracy. While the BJP's supporters celebrate its electoral successes, critics warn that the long-term consequences of its strategies could undermine the diversity and inclusivity that have been the hallmarks of India's political system.

Conclusion

The BJP's political expansion under Narendra Modi has transformed India's political landscape, but not without significant trade-offs. The party's aggressive tactics, including the use of central agencies and the exploitation of leadership vacuums in rival parties, have weakened regional voices and undermined India's pluralism. As the BJP continues to consolidate its power, the challenge for India's democracy will be to preserve its diversity and ensure that the voices of all its communities are heard. Without a strong and united opposition, the risk of India becoming a single-party state, akin to China's political system, looms large. The coming decade will be crucial in determining whether India can reclaim its pluralistic ethos or succumb to the forces of political homogenization.

Governance, Corruption, and Localized Solutions

25. The Promise and Paradox of Anti-Corruption Efforts in Modi's India

26. India's Hidden Battles: Exposing Decades of Strategic Sabotage

27. The Obsolescence of Nation-States: A Case for Localized Governance

৯৹

This section evaluates governance under Modi, the paradox of anti-corruption efforts, and the potential for localized governance in a globalized world.

XXV

The Promise and Paradox of Anti-Corruption Efforts in Modi's India

The 2014 Indian general elections were fundamentally shaped by a powerful anti-corruption sentiment that swept across the nation. The Bharatiya Janata Party (BJP), led by Narendra Modi, capitalized on widespread public frustration with the Congress government's perceived systemic corruption, promising transparency, accountability, and administrative reform. However, the subsequent years have revealed a complex and often contradictory approach to combating corruption that ultimately perpetuates the very system it claimed to dismantle.

❧

Early Promises and Surface-Level Changes

Modi's initial narrative presented a stark contrast to the previous government. By positioning himself as an outsider committed to clean governance, he garnered significant public support. The elimination of high-profile ministerial-level corruption appeared to be a tangible achievement. Yet, this surface-level cleansing masked a deeper, more insidious form of corruption embedded within the governmental machinery.

❧

The Regulatory Paradox

The fundamental flaw in the government's anti-corruption strategy lies in its approach to bureaucratic and regulatory control. Instead of reducing state intervention, Modi's government has paradoxically increased regulatory mechanisms, creating more opportunities for bureaucratic harassment and rent-seeking behaviors. Each new regulation represents not just a rule, but a potential point of extortion, where government officials can exert discretionary power over entrepreneurs and citizens.

❧

Impact on Entrepreneurship

Entrepreneurs have been particularly vulnerable to this systemic challenge. The proliferation of regulations has transformed bureaucratic interactions into potential minefields of corruption. Where once a single clearance might have been required, now multiple layers of approvals create numerous opportunities for informal payments and bureaucratic manipulation. This regulatory labyrinth effectively suffocates entrepreneurial spirit and economic dynamism.

☙

The Bureaucratic Challenge

The government's reliance on the Indian Administrative Service (IAS) officers further compounds the problem. These bureaucrats, traditionally oriented towards state control and centralized decision-making, have been empowered rather than constrained. The result is a continuation of the colonial-era administrative mindset that views regulatory power as an end in itself, rather than a means to facilitate economic and social progress.

☙

Failed Privatization Efforts

Privatization efforts, which could potentially reduce government control and minimize corruption opportunities, have been notably absent. The merger of public sector undertakings (PSUs) has been presented as reform, but it is merely a reshuffling of state-owned entities. True privatization, which would introduce market accountability and reduce bureaucratic discretion, remains conspicuously out of reach.

☙

The Government Control-Corruption Nexus

The relationship between government control and corruption is not coincidental but causal. Each additional regulation, each expansion of bureaucratic discretion, creates new avenues for corrupt practices. The more extensively the state intervenes in economic and social spheres, the more opportunities emerge for extracting bribes, manipulating processes, and exercising unauthorized power.

The Role of Public Awareness

Public awareness is crucial in addressing this systemic issue. Citizens must move beyond superficial anti-corruption rhetoric and understand the structural mechanisms that enable corruption. This requires a nuanced understanding that corruption is not merely about individual moral failings but about institutional design that incentivizes rent-seeking behaviors.

Systemic Solutions

The solution lies not in creating more oversight mechanisms or launching more anti-corruption campaigns, but in fundamentally reimagining the state's role. Reducing regulatory complexity, minimizing bureaucratic discretion, and creating transparent, rule-based systems can significantly mitigate corruption risks.

The Role of Civil Society

Entrepreneurs, civil society organizations, and informed citizens must continuously question and challenge unnecessary regulations. Each regulatory requirement should be scrutinized not just for its stated purpose but for its potential to create corrupt interactions. The goal should be a lean, efficient state that facilitates economic activity rather than controls it.

Missed Opportunities

Modi's government missed a critical opportunity to transform India's governance architecture. While ministerial-level corruption might have been reduced, the underlying systemic issues remain unaddressed. The continued expansion of state control, coupled with increased regulatory complexity, has created a more sophisticated and pervasive form of corruption.

ॐ

The Path Forward

The path forward requires a fundamental philosophical shift. Corruption is not just about individual actions but about institutional design. Reducing government control, simplifying regulations, and creating transparent, rule-based systems are more effective anti-corruption strategies than rhetorical declarations and ministerial musical chairs.

ॐ

Conclusion

For India to truly combat corruption, it must embrace a model of governance that prioritizes individual economic freedom, minimizes state intervention, and creates institutions that are accountable, transparent, and focused on facilitating rather than controlling social and economic interactions.

XXVI

India's Hidden Battles: Exposing Decades of Strategic Sabotage

The story of India's development has been marked not just by challenges of poverty and infrastructure, but by a systematic pattern of external interference aimed at keeping the nation from reaching its full potential.

Technology Sabotage: The SCL Incident and Beyond

The devastating fire at Semiconductor Complex Ltd. (SCL) in Chandigarh in 1989 stands as a stark testament to hidden forces working against India's technological advancement. In 1984, India had achieved remarkable progress in semiconductor technology, advancing from a 5000 nm process to 800 nm in a remarkably short time.

This was a period when neither China nor Taiwan - today's semiconductor powerhouses - had even entered the fabrication space. India was positioned to become a major player in the global semiconductor industry. Then came the mysterious fire of 1989 that completely gutted the complex, setting India's semiconductor progress back by a decade.

This pattern of sabotage extends far beyond the semiconductor industry. The suspicious death of Dr. Homi J. Bhabha, along with several other Indian scientists over the years, points to a coordinated effort to stall India's technological advancement. These weren't random incidents but calculated moves to prevent India from developing crucial technologies that would have established it as a global power decades ago.

Environmental Activism as a Weapon

Environmental activism has often served as a cover for anti-development agendas. The Narmada Dam project, which promised to transform the agricultural and power generation capabilities of multiple states, faced relentless opposition. While legitimate environmental concerns exist, the scale and persistence of these protests, often backed by foreign-funded NGOs, suggest a deeper agenda to prevent India's infrastructure development.

Similar patterns emerge in the opposition to nuclear power projects and mining operations. Under the guise of environmental protection, these movements have effectively delayed critical projects that would have enhanced India's energy security and industrial capabilities. The real cost of these delays isn't just economic - it's the lost potential of what India could have achieved without these systematic obstacles.

৪৩

Religious Warfare: The Two-Pronged Assault

India faces a two-pronged religious assault. From the West, well-funded organizations conduct systematic conversion activities, targeting vulnerable populations and attempting to alter India's demographic composition. Simultaneously, Wahabist elements, supported by Pakistan and other foreign actors, work tirelessly to create insecurity and radicalization among Indian Muslims. This Wahabist infiltration is particularly dangerous as it aims to separate Indian Muslims from their syncretic traditions and push them towards extremist ideologies.

৪৩

The Communist Insurgency Connection

China's support for Maoist insurgencies represents another front in this multi-dimensional warfare. These insurgencies strategically affect mineral-rich areas, preventing India from utilizing its natural resources. The correlation between insurgency-affected areas and regions crucial for India's industrial development is too strong to be coincidental.

৪৩

The Modi Government's Response

The Modi administration has taken decisive action where previous governments remained passive:

- Banned organizations like Greenpeace
- Strengthened FCRA to control foreign funding
- Implemented restrictions on religious conversions

- Controlled NGO activities that mask anti-development agendas
- Pushed back against Wahabist influence through community engagement and security measures

౭౦

Critical Actions for India's Future

India must prioritize:

1. Strengthening counter-intelligence against technology sabotage
2. Monitoring and controlling Wahabist funding and influence operations
3. Scrutinizing environmental activism that targets strategic projects
4. Protecting crucial technology development programs
5. Countering foreign-funded conversion activities
6. Maintaining strict oversight of NGO financing and activities

౭౦

The Stakes and Path Forward

Every successful act of sabotage costs India years, if not decades, of progress. The SCL fire didn't just destroy a facility - it destroyed India's early advantage in semiconductor technology. Similar patterns in nuclear technology, heavy industries, and infrastructure projects have repeatedly delayed India's rise as a global power.

The forces working to undermine India's progress are sophisticated, well-funded, and persistent. They operate through multiple channels - from environmental NGOs to religious organizations, from technology sabotage to insurgency support. The Modi government's recognition of these threats marks a crucial shift in India's approach to national security and development. However, the battle continues as these forces adapt their strategies. India's response must be equally dynamic and resolute. The stakes are too high for anything less than total commitment to countering these threats to national development.

XXVII

The Obsolescence of Nation-States: A Case for Localized Governance

In 48 BCE, as Julius Caesar stood before a statue of Alexander the Great in Spain, he reportedly wept. When asked why, he responded that by his age — 32 years — Alexander had conquered much of the known world, while he himself had achieved "nothing of importance." This moment captures a recurring pattern throughout history: leaders measuring themselves against the towering figures of the past, driven by an almost pathological need to achieve similar glory through conquest and centralized power.

This pursuit of glory through territorial conquest and centralized control, while historically common, has become increasingly anachronistic in our modern world. The nation-state, with its centralized authority and military might, represents an outdated model of governance that continues to perpetuate conflict and instability.

ॐ

The Historical Pattern of Centralized Power

The allure of past glory has consistently driven leaders toward expansionist policies. Napoleon Bonaparte explicitly modeled himself after Caesar and Alexander, dreaming of a unified European empire. Mussolini evoked the Roman Empire to justify his expansionist ambitions. Hitler's Third Reich drew inspiration from an imagined Aryan past. More recently, Vladimir Putin's actions have been partly motivated by nostalgia for Soviet-era influence.

This pattern reveals a fundamental truth: the centralized nation-state model, with its emphasis on territorial control and military power, creates a framework that incentivizes conflict. Leaders inherit not just territory and populations, but historical narratives of past greatness that demand restoration or expansion.

ॐ

The Artificial Nature of Nation-States

The modern nation-state, despite its apparent permanence in our political imagination, is a relatively recent invention. The Peace of Westphalia in 1648 is often cited as the birth of the modern state system, but the nation-state as we know it — with its emphasis on shared language, culture, and identity—truly emerged in the 19th century. This system was never as natural or inevitable as its proponents claimed.

Consider the artificial nature of many national borders, particularly in Africa and Asia, where colonial powers drew lines on maps with little regard for ethnic, linguistic, or cultural realities on the ground. These arbitrary boundaries have been sources of conflict ever since, highlighting the fundamental problem with forcing diverse populations into centralized political units based on European models of statehood.

৪৩

The Inherent Problems of Centralization

The centralized nation-state model suffers from several critical flaws:

1. **Distance from Local Needs**: Centralized governments often fail to understand or address local concerns effectively. A bureaucrat in a distant capital cannot fully grasp the specific needs of diverse communities.
2. **Cultural Homogenization**: Nation-states typically promote a dominant cultural narrative at the expense of regional identities and minorities. This creates internal tensions and resistance.
3. **Military-Industrial Complex**: Centralized states maintain large military forces, which creates a self-perpetuating cycle of arms races and conflict.
4. **Inefficient Resource Allocation**: Central planning often results in inefficient distribution of resources, failing to account for local conditions and needs.

৪৩

The Case for Localization

The alternative to the centralized nation-state is not chaos or isolation, but rather a system of networked local governance that better reflects the realities of our interconnected world. This approach has several advantages:

- **Responsive Governance**: Local governments are better positioned to understand and respond to the specific needs of their communities. When decisions about education, healthcare, infrastructure, and economic development are made at the local level, they can be better tailored to local conditions and preferences.
- **Cultural Preservation**: Localized governance allows for the preservation and celebration of cultural diversity without the homogenizing pressure of national identity. Communities can maintain their unique traditions while still participating in broader networks of trade and cooperation.
- **Environmental Stewardship**: Environmental challenges often require local solutions. While climate change is a global problem, the specific measures needed to address it vary greatly by location. Local governments are better positioned to implement context-appropriate environmental policies.
- **Economic Innovation**: Local governance allows for experimentation with different economic models and policies. Successful approaches can be shared and adapted by other communities, while failed experiments have limited impact.

∞

Learning from Existing Models

Several existing models demonstrate the potential of more localized governance:

Switzerland's canton system provides significant autonomy to local regions while maintaining national coordination where necessary. The European Union, despite its challenges, shows how different political entities can cooperate while maintaining distinct local identities. Indigenous governance systems often provide sophisticated examples of managing resources and making decisions at the local level while maintaining broader networks of cooperation.

৪৩

Gandhi's Vision of Gram Swaraj

Perhaps one of the most compelling models for localized governance comes from Mahatma Gandhi's concept of "gram swaraj" or village self-rule. Gandhi envisioned a decentralized political system where each village would be a self-governing unit, completely capable of managing its own affairs. This was not mere romantic idealization of village life – it was a sophisticated political philosophy that recognized the fundamental problems with centralized power structures.

Gandhi argued that true democracy could only function at the local level, where people have direct control over decisions affecting their lives. He wrote, "Independence must begin at the bottom. Thus, every village will be a republic having full powers." In his vision, villages would be self-sufficient for their basic needs but interdependent for needs they cannot fulfill locally – creating a network of cooperative communities rather than a hierarchical state structure.

The principles of gram swaraj remain remarkably relevant today:

1. **Local Economic Self-Reliance**: Gandhi emphasized local production for local needs, an idea that aligns with

modern concepts of sustainable economics and resilient local economies.

2. **Direct Democracy**: His vision of village assemblies where all adults participate in decision-making offers a model for participatory democracy that modern technology could help scale.

3. **Environmental Sustainability**: The focus on local production and consumption naturally leads to more sustainable resource use, as communities must live within their ecological means.

4. **Social Harmony**: Gandhi believed that local governance would foster better understanding and cooperation between different communities, as people would need to work together to manage shared resources.

While Gandhi's complete vision of village republics may not be directly applicable to our urbanized world, its core principles – decentralization, local autonomy, and participatory democracy – offer valuable guidance for reimagining governance in the 21st century.

൭

The Path Forward

Transitioning from centralized nation-states to more localized governance requires several key steps:

1. **Strengthening Local Democratic Institutions**: Empowering communities to make decisions about their immediate environment and resources.

2. **Developing Inter-Local Cooperation Networks**: Creating frameworks for neighboring regions to collaborate on shared challenges.

3. **Reimagining Security**: Moving from military-based security to cooperative security arrangements between localities.
4. **Preserving Cultural Diversity**: Allowing local communities to maintain their unique identities while participating in global networks.

౮

Conclusion

The age of Alexander, Caesar, and Napoleon – where glory meant territorial conquest and centralized control – must give way to a new understanding of human organization. The future lies not in vast, centralized nation-states but in networked communities of local governance.

The wisdom of Gandhi's gram swaraj reminds us that the push for localization is not a new idea, nor is it simply a reaction against modern problems. Rather, it represents a deep understanding of human nature and the conditions under which people can best govern themselves. As we look for alternatives to the centralized nation-state, these time-tested principles of local self-governance offer both inspiration and practical guidance.

The path forward is clear: we must devolve power to local communities while maintaining the benefits of global connection and cooperation. Only then can we move beyond the ancient cycle of empire, conquest, and conflict that has defined so much of human history.

Global Strategy and India's Role in a Multipolar World

৯

This section explores India's strategic autonomy, its geopolitical challenges, and its role in a shifting global order.

XXVIII

Strategic Autonomy: Navigating Global Power Dynamics in a Multipolar World

In the evolving landscape of global politics, India stands as a pivotal player whose diplomatic choices carry significant weight in shaping international relations. The country's journey from its historical non-alignment stance to its current position of strategic autonomy offers valuable insights into the complexities of modern geopolitics. As the world transitions toward multipolarity, India's ability to balance competing global powers while advancing its national interests has become a defining feature of its international strategy.

The Cold War Legacy: Non-Alignment and Pragmatism

The roots of India's diplomatic balancing act can be traced back to the Cold War era, when despite professing non-alignment, the country found itself gravitating toward the Soviet Union. This alignment manifested in various forms, from the adoption of five-year plans to the implementation of socialist policies that kept the economy relatively closed to foreign influence. The Soviet Union's support during crucial moments, such as the Bangladesh Liberation War, and its role as a primary arms supplier, further cemented this relationship. However, this period also demonstrated the potential limitations of too closely aligning with any single power bloc.

The Post-Liberalization Shift: Embracing Economic and Strategic Realignment

The 1991 economic liberalization under Prime Minister P.V. Narasimha Rao marked a turning point in India's foreign policy. As the country opened its markets to global trade and investment, it began to forge closer ties with the United States. This shift was not without challenges, given the U.S.'s historical support for Pakistan. Nevertheless, India demonstrated remarkable diplomatic dexterity in managing these complexities, signaling its emergence as a more assertive and pragmatic player on the global stage.

Contemporary Diplomacy: Multi-Alignment in a Multipolar World

Under Prime Minister Narendra Modi, India has refined its approach to international relations, embracing a strategy of "multi-alignment." This involves cultivating diverse partnerships across regions and power blocs, from deepening ties with Middle Eastern nations to strengthening traditional relationships with Russia and the West. India's participation in forums like the Quad (with the U.S., Japan, and Australia) and its active role in the BRICS grouping exemplify its ability to engage with competing powers without being tethered to any single alliance. This multi-dimensional diplomacy has proven particularly effective in an era of shifting global power dynamics.

ೞ

Leveraging Economic Strength: A Foundation for Strategic Autonomy

India's growing economic clout is a cornerstone of its strategic autonomy. With one of the world's largest consumer markets, a strategic geographic location, and a rapidly expanding digital economy, India is well-positioned to forge mutually beneficial partnerships. By prioritizing economic collaborations that enhance its technological capabilities and support its development goals, India can strengthen its global influence while maintaining its independence.

ೞ

Building Domestic Capabilities: Reducing External Dependencies

To bolster its strategic autonomy, India must focus on building self-reliance in critical sectors such as defense, technology, and energy. Initiatives like "Make in India" and investments in research and development are steps in the right direction. Reducing reliance on external suppliers not only enhances India's negotiating power but also ensures greater resilience in the face of global disruptions. Policies that foster innovation, infrastructure development, and human capital growth will be essential to achieving this goal.

ॐ

Regional Leadership: Fostering Stability and Growth

As South Asia's largest economy, India has a unique opportunity—and responsibility—to promote regional stability and economic integration. Strengthening ties with neighboring countries through initiatives like the "Neighborhood First" policy and regional connectivity projects can enhance India's influence. Addressing historical tensions, such as those with Pakistan, through sustained diplomatic engagement will be crucial to unlocking the region's full potential and solidifying India's role as a regional leader.

ॐ

Energy Security and Sustainability: A Dual Imperative

India's growing energy demands necessitate a diversified strategy that balances traditional partnerships with Middle Eastern suppliers and investments in renewable energy sources. By prioritizing energy security and environmental sustainability, India can reduce its vulnerability to geopolitical pressures while contributing to global climate goals. This dual approach aligns with India's long-term interests and enhances its credibility as a responsible global actor.

୬

Technology and Digital Sovereignty: Navigating Opportunities and Risks

The technology sector presents both opportunities and challenges for India's strategic autonomy. While partnerships with Western nations can provide access to cutting-edge technologies, concerns over data security and digital sovereignty require careful navigation. India's burgeoning digital economy and skilled workforce position it as a key player in global tech negotiations. However, balancing these partnerships with the need to protect national interests will be critical.

୬

The Path Forward: Strategic Flexibility and Institutional Strength

Looking ahead, India's success in protecting its interests while enhancing its negotiating power will depend on its ability to maintain strategic flexibility while pursuing clear national objectives. This requires sophisticated diplomatic capabilities, strong institutional frameworks, and a clear understanding of long-term national interests. The goal should not be to position India within any particular camp but to maintain the freedom to make strategic choices based on national interests.

୬

Conclusion: Strategic Autonomy in a Multipolar World

India's pursuit of strategic autonomy is not about choosing sides but about preserving the freedom to make decisions that align with its national interests. In an era of multipolarity, this approach allows India to engage productively with all major powers while safeguarding its sovereignty. By leveraging its economic strength, building domestic capabilities, and fostering regional and global partnerships, India can enhance its influence and secure its place as a leading player in the 21st-century world order. The path ahead demands sophisticated diplomacy, clear strategic vision, and an unwavering commitment to India's long-term goals.

XXIX

Strategic Geography: The Afghanistan Link and the Quest for Central Asian Access

India's geographic positioning presents a unique strategic challenge that is often overlooked in conventional analyses of global geopolitics. At the core of this challenge lies a critical corridor—Pakistan-occupied Kashmir (PoK)—which historically connected India to Afghanistan and, by extension, to the resource-rich and strategically vital regions of Central Asia. This geographic reality underscores India's enduring struggle to overcome natural and political barriers to secure access to a region of immense economic and strategic importance.

৪৩

Historical Context and Geographic Realities

Before the partition of the Indian subcontinent in 1947, British India shared a direct border with Afghanistan through the unified territory of Kashmir. This border was more than a line on a map; it was a lifeline for trade, cultural exchange, and strategic movement between South Asia and Central Asia. For centuries, this route facilitated the flow of goods, ideas, and people, linking India to the Silk Road networks that connected Asia to Europe.

The partition of India and the subsequent occupation of parts of Kashmir by Pakistan severed this historic link. Today, PoK stands as a geographic and political barrier, cutting off India's direct land access to Afghanistan and Central Asia. This disruption has had profound implications for India's strategic and economic interests in the region.

৪৩

The Strategic Significance of Pakistan-occupied Kashmir

PoK is not just a disputed territory; it is a potential gateway for India to re-establish its historic connectivity with Afghanistan and Central Asia. If accessible, this corridor would provide India with a direct land route to Central Asian republics such as Turkmenistan, Uzbekistan, and Kazakhstan—nations endowed with vast natural resources, including oil, gas, and minerals, and positioned as key players in regional geopolitics.

The absence of this access has forced India to rely on longer, more circuitous routes to reach Central Asia, limiting its ability to engage economically and strategically with the region. This geographic constraint has also hindered India's capacity to project influence in a region that is increasingly becoming a focal point of global power competition.

ॐ

India's Geographic Constraints: A Peninsula with Island-like Limitations

Despite being a peninsula, India's geographic situation resembles that of an island nation in many ways. To the north, the Himalayas form an imposing natural barrier, while strained political relations with China and Pakistan further restrict land-based connectivity. To the west, Pakistan's control of PoK blocks access to Afghanistan, and to the east, India's northeastern states are geographically isolated by challenging terrain and neighboring countries.

As a result, India's access to Central Asia is effectively constrained, forcing it to depend heavily on maritime routes for trade and strategic engagement. While India has developed robust maritime capabilities, this reliance on sea routes comes with significant limitations, including vulnerability to geopolitical tensions at critical chokepoints like the Strait of Hormuz and the Malacca Strait.

ॐ

The Central Asian Imperative: Energy, Markets, and Strategic Depth

Central Asia holds immense strategic importance for India. The region is a treasure trove of energy resources, which are critical for fueling India's rapidly growing economy. Additionally, Central Asia offers expanding markets for Indian goods, services, and technology, as well as opportunities for infrastructure development and investment.

Beyond economic considerations, Central Asia provides India with strategic depth in an increasingly multipolar world. As China expands its influence through initiatives like the Belt and Road Initiative (BRI) and Russia maintains its historical presence in the region, India's ability to establish a foothold in Central Asia is vital for balancing power dynamics and securing its long-term interests.

Maritime Dependence and Its Limitations

While India has made significant strides in developing its maritime infrastructure and forging international partnerships, exclusive reliance on sea routes is not without challenges. Maritime transportation is inherently slower, more expensive, and susceptible to disruptions caused by piracy, geopolitical tensions, and environmental factors. Moreover, India's dependence on key maritime chokepoints exposes it to risks that could undermine its energy security and trade flows.

The Way Forward: Overcoming Geographic Constraints

India has undertaken several initiatives to mitigate its geographic limitations and enhance connectivity with Central Asia. The development of Iran's Chabahar Port, for instance, provides India with a strategic foothold in the region and an alternative route to Afghanistan and beyond. Similarly, India's investment in the International North-South Transport Corridor (INSTC)—a multimodal network linking India to Russia via Iran and Central Asia—aims to reduce transit times and costs for trade.

Diplomatic engagement with Central Asian nations has also been a priority, with India hosting the India-Central Asia Summit and deepening ties in areas such as defense, energy, and technology. However, while these efforts are commendable, they cannot fully compensate for the strategic advantage that direct land access through PoK would offer.

✷

Conclusion: Geography as Destiny

India's geographic realities underscore the importance of connectivity in shaping its strategic and economic future. The nation's efforts to overcome its constraints—through infrastructure development, diplomatic engagement, and regional partnerships—reflect a clear understanding of the critical role geography plays in global power dynamics.

As India continues to navigate an increasingly complex geopolitical landscape, the restoration of its historic links to Central Asia remains a strategic imperative. Whether through innovative solutions or diplomatic breakthroughs, India's ability to secure reliable access to this vital region will be a key determinant of its rise as a global power. Understanding this geographic reality is essential for appreciating India's strategic challenges and the opportunities that lie ahead.

XXX

India's Geopolitical Balancing Act in South Asia

India faces a complex geopolitical challenge in South Asia, where it must navigate relationships with smaller neighboring countries that often view it with suspicion. This dynamic is common throughout world history—smaller nations frequently harbor resentment toward larger regional powers, perceiving them as potential threats to sovereignty. For India, maintaining influence in these neighboring states isn't merely about power projection; it represents a fundamental national security imperative that requires constant vigilance and, when necessary, direct intervention to safeguard its interests.

☙

The Buffer State Concept in South Asian Geopolitics

Many of India's neighbors were established as buffer states—territories designed to separate larger powers and reduce direct confrontation. Nepal, Bhutan, and Myanmar historically served as buffers between British India and China, while Pakistan emerged from the partition of 1947 partly to create separation between India and Afghanistan. These buffer arrangements have evolved into modern nation-states, but India must maintain strategic control over them to prevent hostile powers from gaining footholds that could threaten Indian security.

Economic and Security Dimensions of Regional Control

India's interest in its neighborhood extends beyond traditional security concerns. By establishing economic dependency relationships, India creates leverage that can be used to ensure political compliance from neighboring regimes. This approach requires substantial investment but yields significant returns in terms of strategic influence. When economic ties prove insufficient to maintain favorable governments, India must be prepared to employ more direct methods of intervention to protect its regional interests.

The Chinese Challenge to India's Regional Influence

China's engagement with South Asian countries represents a direct challenge to India's traditional sphere of influence. The Hambantota Port in Sri Lanka stands as a clear warning—initially developed with Chinese loans, it was eventually leased to China for 99 years, effectively establishing a Chinese naval presence near India's southern flank. India cannot afford similar strategic encirclements and must take decisive action to counter Chinese initiatives, including supporting regime changes when governments become excessively pro-Chinese.

ॐ

Great Power Competition in India's Backyard

The geopolitical landscape of South Asia is further complicated by the involvement of external powers, particularly the United States and China. Both powers view the region through their broader strategic competition, with Pakistan particularly serving as a battleground for influence. While China strengthens its "all-weather friendship" with Pakistan through initiatives like the China-Pakistan Economic Corridor (CPEC), the United States has historically maintained military and economic ties with Pakistan while simultaneously pursuing a strategic partnership with India.

India must strategically manage these relationships, leveraging American support when it aligns with Indian interests while firmly countering Chinese encroachment. This requires sophisticated intelligence operations and the cultivation of reliable proxies in neighboring countries who can advance Indian interests even when public diplomacy must remain restrained.

ॐ

Myanmar: A Critical Frontier Requiring Direct Management

Myanmar represents one of India's most strategically significant neighbors, sharing a 1,643-kilometer border with India's northeastern states. The country serves as India's land bridge to Southeast Asia and is vital for the success of India's "Act East" policy. China's deep economic and military ties with Myanmar threaten India's security by potentially allowing hostile forces to operate from Myanmar's territory. India must maintain robust intelligence networks within Myanmar and be prepared to support political forces that align with Indian interests, even if this means working toward changes in Myanmar's government when necessary.

ॐ

The Maldives, Nepal and Bhutan: Strategic Competition in Small States

Even small states like the Maldives hold outsized strategic significance due to their location in the Indian Ocean. Similarly, Nepal's position between India and China makes controlling its government a critical objective for Indian security. In Bhutan, India has established a model of effective strategic management that should be replicated elsewhere, maintaining de facto control over Bhutan's foreign and defense policies. These examples demonstrate both the possibility and necessity of maintaining strategic dominance over smaller neighbors.

ॐ

The Bangladesh Case Study: Shifting Political Alignments

The Bangladesh situation exemplifies the fragility of India's regional influence when faced with sudden political transitions. The ousting of Sheikh Hasina's government in August 2024 after fifteen years in power has fundamentally altered India's strategic position along its eastern border. This change, reportedly influenced by Western foundations including those associated with Hillary Clinton and George Soros, represents a potentially significant realignment in

Bangladesh's orientation.

The interim government under Mohammad Yunus has made decisions with profound security implications for India, including lifting bans on Islamist organizations and releasing detained leaders with anti-India histories. Reports of violence against Hindu minorities have further complicated bilateral relations. As Bangladesh moves toward elections tentatively scheduled for late 2025, the potential resurgence of Khaleda Zia's Bangladesh Nationalist Party introduces additional uncertainties against the backdrop of increasing Chinese economic engagement.

India now faces the challenge of recalibrating its approach without triggering international backlash or strengthening anti-India sentiment within Bangladesh. This requires developing multidimensional engagement strategies that maintain influence through economic leverage, cultural connections, and intelligence capabilities while adapting to new political realities. The situation underscores the necessity of maintaining diverse channels of influence that can withstand political transitions and developing early warning systems for political instability rather than relying exclusively on incumbent leadership relationships.

ॐ

Afghanistan: The Outer Ring of Strategic Concern

Though not sharing a direct border with India since Partition, Afghanistan remains crucial to India's strategic calculus. The Taliban takeover in 2021 represented a significant setback for Indian interests and a corresponding gain for Pakistan. India must develop a long-term strategy for Afghanistan that:

1. Develops channels to pragmatic elements within the Taliban
2. Uses economic and development leverage to maintain influence
3. Prevents Afghanistan from becoming a sanctuary for anti-India terrorist groups

ॐ

The Seychelles and Mauritius: Extended Maritime Neighbors

In the Indian Ocean realm, both Seychelles and Mauritius represent important partners for India's maritime security strategy. China's attempts to establish presence in these island nations directly threatens India's position in the Indian Ocean. India's development of military facilities in Seychelles (Assumption Island) and support for Mauritius must continue with increased vigor.

ॐ

The Techniques of Regional Control

Effective regional dominance operates through multiple channels—economic assistance, cultural diplomacy, political support for friendly regimes, intelligence operations, and occasionally more direct intervention. When neighboring governments drift toward anti-India positions, India must be prepared to implement regime change operations through a combination of economic pressure, support for opposition groups, and covert action.

ॐ

The Necessity of Proactive Strategic Management

India cannot afford to be passive or reactive in its neighborhood policy. The stakes are too high, and competitors—particularly China—are too active. While respecting international norms, India must:

1. Maintain robust intelligence networks throughout neighboring countries
2. Identify and support pro-India political forces
3. When necessary, work discreetly toward political change in countries where leadership has become hostile to Indian interests
4. Use economic leverage through targeted development assistance
5. Develop military ties that create dependency relationships

ॐ

The Imperative of Vigilant Control

For India, maintaining tight vigilance and control over neighboring governments is not a choice but a strategic necessity. When governments in these nations drift toward hostility or alignment with rival powers, particularly China, India must be prepared to take decisive action. This may include supporting opposition movements, applying economic pressure, or utilizing intelligence capabilities to facilitate regime change. The costs of failing to maintain this control—in terms of national security, economic interests, and regional stability—far outweigh the diplomatic risks of intervention.

ॐ

Strategic Realism and Assertive Approach

India's neighborhood policy must be guided by strategic realism rather than idealism. The fundamental principle should be that friendly governments in neighboring countries are essential to India's national security. When regimes tilt decisively against Indian interests or toward hostile powers, India must be prepared to use all elements of national power—diplomatic, informational, military, and economic—to restore a favorable balance.

The rise of China and the potential for increased great power competition in South Asia means that traditional restraint may no longer serve India's interests. A more assertive approach to regional management, particularly regarding regime orientation in key neighbors, represents an uncomfortable but necessary adaptation to changing geopolitical realities.

India's regional strategy requires sophisticated mechanisms of control that ensure neighboring governments remain aligned with Indian interests. When diplomatic and economic tools prove insufficient, India must be prepared to help engineer political changes in these countries. This approach recognizes that in the harsh reality of geopolitics, buffer states must function as extensions of India's security perimeter rather than truly independent entities. As competition with China intensifies, India's capacity to maintain—and when necessary, restore—favorable political alignments in neighboring countries will determine its success as a regional power and its security as a nation.

XXXI

Cultural Influence vs. Territorial Expansion

In an age of interconnected economies and soft power diplomacy, the concept of Akhand Bharat (unified India) represents an outdated approach to national influence. While the historical idea of a culturally unified Indian subcontinent holds emotional appeal for some, pursuing territorial expansion in modern times would be both impractical and counterproductive. Instead, India's path to global influence lies in leveraging its rich cultural heritage, spiritual traditions, and economic potential.

৪৩

The Current Western Embrace

India's cultural impact is already evident in the Western world, where practices like yoga, meditation, and Ayurveda have become mainstream. This organic spread of Indian cultural elements demonstrates the power of soft influence over territorial control. Yoga studios can be found in virtually every major Western city, with millions of practitioners embracing not just the physical aspects but also the underlying philosophical principles. Similarly, Ayurvedic medicine and wellness practices have gained recognition in global healthcare discussions, offering alternative approaches to health and healing.

The West's fascination with Indian spirituality and wellness is not merely a trend but a reflection of a deeper search for meaning in an increasingly fragmented world. India's ability to export these practices without coercion or political pressure demonstrates the universal appeal of its cultural heritage.

ॐ

Spiritual and Philosophical Heritage

India's spiritual and philosophical traditions offer timeless wisdom that resonates with contemporary global challenges. The Bhagavad Gita, with its teachings on duty, purpose, and self-realization, speaks to modern seekers grappling with questions of identity and fulfillment. The Upanishads and Vedas, with their profound insights into consciousness and reality, align with cutting-edge discussions in psychology, neuroscience, and quantum physics. These ancient texts provide not just philosophical depth but also practical solutions to modern issues like stress, alienation, and the search for meaning.

By reframing these teachings in accessible, contemporary formats, India can position itself as a global thought leader. Imagine apps that distill Vedic wisdom into daily mindfulness practices, or online courses that explore the Bhagavad Gita through the lens of modern leadership.

The potential for cultural influence is immense, provided India can modernize its delivery without diluting its essence.

ॐ

Literary and Narrative Power

India's literary heritage is a treasure trove of universal themes and compelling narratives. The epics Ramayana and Mahabharata explore timeless concepts of duty, justice, family, and moral choice, rivaling the dramatic power of Greek mythology. The Panchatantra, with its animal fables, has already demonstrated cross-cultural appeal, having been translated into over 50 languages over centuries.

These stories could be reimagined for modern audiences through films, television series, video games, and graphic novels. Imagine a Mahabharata-inspired series with the production quality of Game of Thrones, or a Panchatantra-themed animated franchise for children. By leveraging its narrative wealth, India can captivate global audiences while preserving and propagating its cultural values.

ॐ

The Success of Indian Cuisine: A Model for Cultural Expansion

The global popularity of Indian cuisine offers a blueprint for cultural influence. Without government intervention, Indian food has become a staple worldwide, with dishes like curry being integrated into national cuisines from Britain to Japan. This organic spread, driven by inherent appeal rather than political pressure, exemplifies the most sustainable form of cultural influence.

ॐ

Heritage Sites and Historical Legacy

India's UNESCO World Heritage sites, from the Taj Mahal to the temples of Khajuraho, are not just tourist attractions but powerful symbols of its historical and cultural legacy. The ancient urban centers of the Indus Valley Civilization, such as Dholavira and Lothal, showcase India's early contributions to urban planning and civil engineering. By preserving and promoting these sites, India can strengthen its cultural diplomacy and attract global interest in its history and achievements.

※

Economic Development Priority

For India to fully realize its cultural potential, it must first address its domestic challenges. With a per capita GDP significantly lower than China's $12,500, India's priority must be economic development, poverty reduction, and infrastructure improvement. A prosperous, well-educated population will naturally become more effective ambassadors of Indian culture and values.

Investing in education, technology, and innovation will not only uplift millions but also enhance India's global standing. The resources that might otherwise be wasted on territorial ambitions should be channeled into building a knowledge-based economy that can compete on the world stage.

※

Learning from China's Playbook

China's rise to global influence offers valuable lessons. Rather than pursuing territorial expansion, China has focused on economic strength and cultural exports, from Confucius Institutes to its booming film industry. India, with its rich spiritual and philosophical traditions, has an even greater opportunity to shape global discourse. However, it must present its cultural offerings in accessible, contemporary formats while maintaining their authenticity.

❧

A Strategic Vision for Cultural Diplomacy

Instead of pursuing the anachronistic dream of Akhand Bharat, India should develop a comprehensive cultural diplomacy strategy. This could include:

- **Academic Research and Translations**: Supporting scholarly work to make classical texts accessible to global audiences.
- **Promoting Performing Arts**: Showcasing Indian dance, music, and theater on international platforms.
- **Cultural Exchange Programs**: Strengthening ties through student and professional exchanges.
- Digital Platforms: Creating online hubs to share Indian knowledge systems, from Ayurveda to Vedic mathematics.
- **Modernizing Traditions**: Adapting ancient practices for contemporary lifestyles while preserving their essence.
- **Intellectual Property Protection**: Safeguarding traditional knowledge from exploitation.

❧

The Path Forward

The success of Indian cuisine worldwide offers a model for cultural expansion. Without any governmental push, Indian food has become popular globally, with curry being adopted into national cuisines from Britain to Japan. This organic spread of cultural elements, driven by their inherent appeal rather than political pressure, represents the most sustainable form of influence.

&

Conclusion: A Future Built on Ideas, Not Borders

The concept of Akhand Bharat belongs to the past. In today's world, cultural influence far outweighs the benefits of territorial control. India's vast spiritual, philosophical, and artistic heritage provides the tools to shape global discourse and offer solutions to modern challenges. By focusing on economic development, cultural diplomacy, and innovation, India can achieve genuine global impact while improving the lives of its citizens. The future lies not in occupying lands but in occupying minds and hearts through the timeless appeal of Indian wisdom and culture.

In the words of Swami Vivekananda, "All power is within you; you can do anything and everything." India's power lies not in its borders but in its ideas—and the world is ready to listen.

XXXII

The Diaspora Dilemma: How NRIs Are Shaping India's Global Image and Domestic Politics

The Indian diaspora, one of the largest and most influential in the world, has become a critical force in shaping India's global image, economic policies, and even its domestic politics. With over 32 million people of Indian origin living abroad, the diaspora wields significant economic, cultural, and political clout. From lobbying for India's interests on the global stage to funding political campaigns at home, the diaspora's role is both multifaceted and complex. However, this influence is not without its contradictions and tensions, as the diaspora's idealized vision of India often clashes with the realities on the ground.

ॐ

Modi's Diaspora Diplomacy: Political and Economic Motivations

Prime Minister Narendra Modi has been particularly adept at engaging with the Indian diaspora, leveraging their influence to bolster India's global standing and domestic agenda. Events like the "Howdy Modi" rally in Houston, Texas, in 2019, where Modi addressed a crowd of over 50,000 Indian-Americans alongside then-U.S. President Donald Trump, exemplify this strategy. These events serve dual purposes: they reinforce Modi's image as a global leader and strengthen ties with the diaspora, who are seen as key stakeholders in India's development.

The political motivations behind Modi's outreach are clear. The diaspora is a valuable source of financial support for political campaigns, both in India and abroad. Many Indian-Americans, for instance, have donated to U.S. political candidates who align with India's interests, thereby influencing foreign policy. Economically, the diaspora is a critical source of remittances, which totaled over $100 billion in 2022, making India the largest recipient of remittances globally. These funds not only support families back home but also contribute to India's foreign exchange reserves, stabilizing the economy.

ॐ

Shaping Global Perceptions: The Diaspora and Hindu Nationalism

The diaspora has played a significant role in shaping global perceptions of India, particularly in the context of Hindu nationalism. Many members of the diaspora, especially those who identify strongly with their Hindu heritage, have become vocal advocates for Modi's Bharatiya Janata Party (BJP) and its Hindutva ideology. Organizations like the Vishwa Hindu Parishad (VHP) and the Hindu Swayamsevak Sangh (HSS) have established a strong presence abroad, promoting a narrative of India as a Hindu nation.

This advocacy has had a polarizing effect. While it has galvanized support for India among certain segments of the global population, it has also led to criticism, particularly from those who view Hindutva as exclusionary and divisive. The diaspora's role in amplifying Hindu nationalist rhetoric has, in some cases, exacerbated tensions between India and other countries, particularly those with significant Muslim populations.

ಔ

The Idealized India vs. Ground Realities

One of the most striking aspects of the diaspora's influence is the tension between their idealized vision of India and the realities on the ground. For many members of the diaspora, India represents a cultural and spiritual homeland, a place of ancient traditions and values. This idealized image often overlooks the complexities and challenges of contemporary India, including issues of poverty, caste discrimination, and religious tensions.

This disconnect can lead to a form of cultural nostalgia that is out of sync with the lived experiences of those in India. For instance, while the diaspora may celebrate India's economic growth and technological advancements, they may be less aware of the social inequalities that persist. This gap between perception and reality can sometimes result in misguided policies or investments that fail to address the root causes of India's challenges.

෫

Diaspora Remittances and India's Development Trajectory

The economic impact of the diaspora cannot be overstated. Remittances from overseas Indians are a lifeline for millions of families, particularly in states like Kerala, Punjab, and Gujarat. These funds are used for education, healthcare, and housing, significantly improving the quality of life for recipients. Beyond remittances, the diaspora has also been a key driver of foreign direct investment (FDI) in India, particularly in sectors like IT, real estate, and manufacturing.

However, the reliance on remittances also raises questions about India's long-term economic sustainability. While these funds provide immediate relief, they do not necessarily translate into sustainable development. There is a need for more strategic investments that create jobs and foster innovation, rather than simply relying on the generosity of the diaspora.

෫

Escaping India: The Diaspora's Resentment and Influence

Not all members of the diaspora view India through a lens of nostalgia or pride. For some, leaving India was a means of escaping social, economic, or political oppression. Lower-caste individuals, for instance, have used education as a pathway to move abroad, seeking to escape the caste-based humiliation they faced in India. Similarly, many

Sikhs emigrated following the anti-Sikh riots of 1984, harboring deep resentment against the Indian state and, in some cases, against Hinduism and Hindutva.

These sections of the diaspora have become influential in shaping global perceptions of India, often in ways that challenge the dominant narrative. In countries like Canada, where the Sikh diaspora is particularly strong, this has led to tensions in bilateral relations. The Canadian government's criticism of India's human rights record, particularly in relation to Sikh issues, has been influenced by the activism of the Sikh diaspora. This highlights the dual role of the diaspora as both a bridge and a barrier in India's international relations.

ॐ

Diaspora Influence on Domestic Politics: The Farmers' Agitation

The Indian diaspora's influence is not limited to global perceptions; it also extends to domestic politics. A recent example is the farmers' agitation of 2020-2021, which saw widespread protests against the Indian government's agricultural reforms. The diaspora played a significant role in amplifying the farmers' cause on the global stage, organizing rallies, lobbying foreign governments, and using social media to draw international attention to the issue.

This activism had a tangible impact, with celebrities and politicians abroad expressing solidarity with the protesters. The Indian government, in turn, accused the diaspora of misrepresenting the situation and undermining India's sovereignty. This episode highlights the diaspora's ability to influence domestic politics, often in ways that challenge the official narrative.

ॐ

Conclusion: The Dual Role of the Diaspora

The Indian diaspora is a powerful force, shaping India's global image and domestic politics in profound ways. Through their economic contributions, political advocacy, and cultural influence, they have become key players in India's development trajectory. However, their influence is not without its challenges. The tension between the diaspora's idealized vision of India and the realities on the ground, as well as the divergent experiences of different sections of the diaspora, create a complex dynamic that India must navigate carefully.

As India continues to rise on the global stage, the role of the diaspora will only become more significant. Understanding and addressing the diaspora's diverse perspectives and motivations will be crucial for India to harness their potential effectively. Whether as ambassadors, investors, or critics, the diaspora will remain at the heart of India's ongoing story, shaping its future in ways that are both visible and unseen.

Legacy and the Future

33. The Looming Succession: Modi's Legacy and the Power Brokers Behind India's Political Landscape

34. The Digital Revolution in Indian Political Discourse

This section looks ahead to Modi's legacy, the digital revolution in politics, and the looming succession battle.

XXXIII

The Looming Succession: Modi's Legacy and the Power Brokers Behind India's Political Landscape

As Prime Minister Narendra Modi approaches the later stages of his political career, the question of succession within the Bharatiya Janata Party (BJP) has become a topic of intense speculation and strategic maneuvering. At 74 years old, Modi's eventual retirement presents a critical juncture for both the party and the powerful business interests that have been instrumental in shaping his political trajectory.

ॐ

The Media and Social Narrative

The narrative of Modi's rise to national prominence is intrinsically linked to the strategic support of two of India's most influential business conglomerates: the Ambani and Adani groups. Their role in Modi's political ascension goes far beyond traditional corporate-political relationships, representing a symbiotic partnership that has fundamentally transformed India's political and economic landscape.

During Modi's initial push for national leadership, these corporate giants played a pivotal role in manufacturing his nationwide narrative. Social media platforms and extensive media campaigns carefully crafted an image of Modi as a transformative leader, capable of bringing unprecedented economic growth and development to India. The technological and financial muscle of Ambani and Adani's media and communication networks proved instrumental in creating a pan-national support base that transcended regional and traditional political boundaries.

ॐ

Economic Transformations and Corporate Interests

Upon assuming power in 2014, Modi did not merely reciprocate the support – he systematically created an ecosystem that significantly benefited these corporate allies. The Adani Group's meteoric rise is perhaps the most striking example of this mutual relationship. Following Modi's ascension, Adani's market capitalization witnessed an extraordinary expansion, with the group securing crucial infrastructure projects across multiple sectors, including ports, power, and logistics.

The government's policy decisions further illuminated this intricate relationship. Modifications to Foreign Direct Investment (FDI) rules effectively curtailed the expansion of global retail giants like Amazon and Walmart, simultaneously creating more favorable conditions for domestic corporate entities. This strategic intervention was perceived by many as a clear demonstration of the government's preference for specific business interests.

Navigating Controversies

Controversies surrounding these relationships have been persistent but largely ineffective in challenging the established narrative. The Hindenburg Research report, which raised serious questions about the Adani Group's financial practices, failed to generate sustained political or regulatory pressure. Similarly, allegations of corruption in state-level transactions, such as those involving the Andhra Pradesh government, were systematically sidelined.

The Succession Landscape

As the discourse around Modi's succession gains momentum, potential successors are being carefully evaluated not just on their political acumen, but on their ability to maintain these crucial corporate relationships. Amit Shah emerges as a frontrunner, given his close proximity to Modi and proven organizational capabilities. While other leaders like Nitin Gadkari might enjoy support from the Rashtriya Swayamsevak Sangh (RSS), the ultimate validation will likely come from the corporate power centers that have defined the Modi era.

Requirements for the Next Leader

The successor will need to demonstrate not just political skill, but a willingness to continue the established model of corporate-political collaboration. The next leader must prove capable of maintaining the delicate balance between national narrative, corporate interests, and political strategy that has characterized the Modi government.

Yogi Adityanath, often speculated as a potential successor, presents an interesting case. While he commands significant ideological support and has demonstrated administrative capabilities in Uttar Pradesh, his selection would require the explicit approval of both the party's core leadership and its corporate stakeholders.

A New Political Ecosystem

What becomes increasingly clear is that the succession is not merely a political transition, but a carefully choreographed process involving multiple stakeholders. The corporate endorsement, particularly from groups like Ambani and Adani, will be crucial in determining the next national leadership.

This model of political succession represents a sophisticated evolution of India's political ecosystem. It goes beyond traditional power brokering, embedding corporate interests deeply within the political machinery. The next leader will be expected to continue this approach, maintaining a delicate balance between national rhetoric, economic expansion, and corporate partnerships.

Conclusion: A Delicate Balance

As India approaches this critical political transition, the selection of Modi's successor will reveal much about the future of the BJP and the broader political-corporate ecosystem. The chosen leader must navigate a complex landscape of ideological expectations, party dynamics, and corporate interests.

The world will be watching closely. The succession will not just determine the next leader of the world's largest democracy, but will provide crucial insights into the intricate power structures that define contemporary Indian politics.

XXXIV

The Digital Revolution in Indian Political Discourse

The recent announcement by Finance Minister Nirmala Sitharaman regarding the dramatic overhaul of personal income tax structures marks a significant moment in Indian governance - not just for the policy change itself, but for how it came to be. The decision, influenced by widespread social media discourse about tax burdens, exemplifies how digital platforms have become powerful catalysts for policy change in modern India.

From Streets to Screens: The Evolution of Public Protest

The traditional image of Indian political movements often featured massive rallies, with party workers laboriously organizing crowds to demonstrate strength in numbers. These gatherings, while historically significant, often involved what critics termed as "rent-a-crowd" phenomena, where participants were sometimes transported to venues without full engagement with the issues at hand. This approach, increasingly viewed as anachronistic, is giving way to a more organic, digitally-driven form of public participation.

ॐ

Social Media: The New Public Square

The transformation of public discourse through social media has democratized political participation in unprecedented ways. Unlike traditional protests that required physical presence and often substantial organizational resources, social media platforms enable citizens to voice their opinions, share grievances, and mobilize support from the comfort of their homes. This digital revolution has made political participation more accessible, immediate, and measurable.

ॐ

Case Studies in Digital Influence

The power of social media in Indian politics has been demonstrated repeatedly. The Anna Hazare anti-corruption movement of 2011-12 marked one of the first major instances where social media amplified a grassroots campaign to national prominence. The movement's success in mobilizing public opinion through digital platforms set a precedent for future political activism.

Another notable example was the controversy surrounding Prime Minister Narendra Modi's personalized suit, which featured his name woven into the fabric. What might have been a minor fashion faux pas in an earlier era became a significant political issue as images spread rapidly across social media platforms, leading to widespread criticism and political consequences for the BJP.

ॐ

The Tax Reform Movement: A Digital-Age Victory

The recent tax reform announcement, removing tax obligations for annual incomes up to 1.2 million rupees, represents perhaps the most concrete example of social media's influence on policy-making. The sustained digital discourse about tax burdens, coupled with the ability to share personal stories and data across platforms, created a compelling narrative that the government could not ignore.

ॐ

Advantages of Digital Activism

Digital movements offer several distinct advantages over traditional forms of political organization:

1. **Authenticity**: Online movements tend to reflect genuine public sentiment more accurately than orchestrated physical gatherings.
2. **Cost-effectiveness**: Digital campaigns require minimal financial resources compared to organizing physical protests.
3. **Data-driven feedback**: Governments can gauge public opinion more precisely through social media analytics.
4. **Rapid scalability**: Issues can quickly gain national attention if they resonate with the public.

ॐ

Challenges and Considerations

However, the digital transformation of political discourse isn't without its challenges. The rise of misinformation, echo chambers, and algorithmic bias can distort public debate. The digital divide in India also means that social media movements might not fully represent all segments of society, particularly rural and economically disadvantaged populations.

৪৩

The Future of Political Engagement

The success of social media in influencing the recent tax reforms suggests a growing trend where digital platforms will play an increasingly crucial role in policy-making. This shift represents a more sophisticated form of democracy, where public opinion can be expressed and measured in real-time, leading to more responsive governance.

৪৩

Implications for Democratic Processes

This evolution in political discourse has several implications for Indian democracy:

1. Political parties must adapt their communication strategies to engage effectively on digital platforms.
2. Policy-makers need to develop better mechanisms for incorporating social media feedback into governance.
3. Citizens must become more digitally literate to participate effectively in these new forums of democracy.

৪৩

Conclusion

The recent tax reforms, influenced by social media discourse, represent more than just a policy change - they signal a fundamental shift in how democracy functions in the digital age. The days of herding crowds to demonstrate political strength are giving way to more nuanced, digital forms of public participation. This transformation, while presenting its own challenges, offers the potential for more responsive, efficient, and authentic democratic engagement.

As India continues to lead in digital adoption, the influence of social media on policy-making is likely to grow stronger. The success of the tax reform movement demonstrates that when citizens effectively utilize digital platforms to voice their concerns, significant policy changes can result. This new paradigm of political engagement, combining the reach of digital platforms with genuine grassroots sentiment, may well become the standard model for future political movements in India.

India's Unresolved Contradictions: A Path Forward

India's journey through the Modi era has laid bare a series of fundamental contradictions that will shape its trajectory for decades to come. The themes explored throughout this book – from the interplay of religious nationalism and economic reform to the persistence of socialist mindsets amid market liberalization – reveal a nation grappling with competing visions of its future while carrying the weight of its past.

༅

Political Power vs. Economic Reform

The first major contradiction lies in the relationship between political consolidation and economic transformation. The BJP's dominance under Modi has created unprecedented political stability at the national level, theoretically providing the perfect conditions for bold economic reforms. Yet this very consolidation of power has paradoxically reduced the impetus for systemic change. The government's strength has allowed it to manage the existing system rather than transform it, leading to selective reforms that work within the framework of state control rather than fundamentally challenging it.

༅

Social Cohesion and Economic Progress

A second contradiction emerges in the realm of social cohesion and economic progress. While the government has successfully mobilized a Hindu nationalist narrative that resonates with large sections of the population, this has come at the cost of increasing economic marginalization of minorities, particularly Muslims. The resulting social tensions create inefficiencies and barriers to growth that undermine India's economic potential. The question remains whether national unity built on cultural dominance can provide the stable foundation needed for sustained economic development.

The Socialist Legacy

The persistence of socialist ideas in Indian political discourse presents a third contradiction. Despite three decades of liberalization and clear evidence of market-driven growth's potential, India's public sphere remains dominated by non-market participants who view state control as the solution to economic challenges. This ideological environment makes it difficult to build popular support for crucial reforms in areas like labor laws, privatization, and land acquisition.

Charting a New Course

Looking forward, India's path to resolving these contradictions will require several fundamental shifts. First, the country needs to recognize that genuine economic reform and social harmony are mutually reinforcing rather than competing goals. A truly dynamic economy requires the full participation of all communities, while economic opportunity can help heal social divisions.

Second, India must move beyond the false choice between state control and market chaos. The experience of successful Asian economies shows that effective state capacity and market mechanisms can work in tandem. Rather than defending or dismantling the existing system of state control, India needs to reimagine the role of government as an enabler of market-driven growth while ensuring inclusive development.

ॐ

Critical Challenges Ahead

The upcoming decade will be crucial in determining whether India can navigate these contradictions successfully. The country's demographic dividend provides a narrow window of opportunity, but harnessing it will require addressing several critical challenges:

1. The banking sector and credit markets must be modernized to support entrepreneurship and innovation, particularly among smaller businesses and traditionally disadvantaged groups.
2. Anti-corruption efforts need to move beyond high-profile actions to focus on systematic reforms that reduce opportunities for rent-seeking while preserving necessary state capacity.
3. The political system must evolve to allow for healthy competition of ideas while maintaining stability, avoiding both single-party dominance and fragmentary opposition.
4. Social reforms must create genuine opportunities for economic mobility while respecting India's cultural and religious diversity.

ॐ

Beyond Binary Choices

The path forward requires acknowledging that India's contradictions cannot be resolved through simple choices between competing extremes. Instead, progress will come through carefully crafted synthesis – finding ways to preserve social stability while promoting change, maintaining cultural identity while embracing diversity, and leveraging state capacity while unleashing market forces.

A Transformative Moment

Success in this endeavor will require political leadership that can rise above immediate electoral calculations to focus on long-term transformation. It will also demand an engaged citizenry willing to move beyond ideological positions to support practical solutions. Most importantly, it will require recognition that India's greatest strength lies not in enforced uniformity but in its ability to embrace and synthesize seemingly contradictory forces into a dynamic whole.

The choices made in the coming years will determine whether India can transform its contradictions from sources of tension into drivers of progress. The stakes could not be higher – not just for India's 1.4 billion citizens, but for the future of democratic development in an increasingly complex world.